The Liberty Bell

Gary B. Nash

Set in Janson type by Integrated Publishing Solutions.

The Library of Congress has catalogued the hardcover edition as follows:

Nash, Gary B.
The Liberty Bell / Gary B. Nash
p. cm. — (Icons of America)
Includes bibliographical references and index.
ISBN 978-0-300-13936-5 (cloth : alk paper)   1. Liberty Bell.
2. Philadelphia (Pa.)—Buildings, structures, etc.   I. Title.
F158.8.I3N37 2010
973—dc22   2009041617
ISBN 978-0-300-17142-6 (pbk.)

A catalogue record for this book
is available from the British Library.

10 9 8 7 6 5 4 3 2 1

The Liberty Bell

Yale UNIVERSITY PRESS   NEW HAVEN & LONDON

ICONS OF AMERICA

Mark Crispin Miller, Series Editor

Icons of America is a series of short works written by leading scholars, critics, and writers, each of whom tells a new and innovative story about American history and culture through the lens of a single iconic individual, event, object, or cultural phenomenon.

For my grandchildren,
Chessie, Nicholas, Mary Brooke, Colin, Lee,
Liliane, Lindsay, Julian, and Ben

Contents

Introduction

It is America's most famous relic, a nearly sacred totem. Several million people each year make a pilgrimage to see it, often dabbing their eyes as they gaze at it intently.

Everywhere around the world it is regarded as a universal symbol of freedom. As icons go, there's nothing quite like it short of the Rosetta Stone or the Holy Grail.

It began inconspicuously; it nearly ended up in the scrap heap; it cracked and lost its voice; it was all but forgotten. But then, gradually, it became a priceless national treasure.

The Liberty Bell is only a sliver of American history. But few slivers have had such resonance. For more than a century, the Liberty Bell has captured Americans' affections and become a stand-in for the nation's vaunted values: independence, freedom, unalienable rights, and equality. It is virtually a touchstone of American identity because Americans have adopted it, along with the flag, as the symbol of justice, the rule of law, and the guardian of sovereign rights.

In fact, the Liberty Bell found its way into the hearts of most American schoolchildren before the Stars and Stripes stood at the front of their classrooms. Not until 1892 did a Baptist minister compose the pledge of allegiance to the American flag and publish it in a family-oriented magazine. After that the pledge took effect only gradually. The "Star-Spangled Banner" was rarely sung anywhere in the United States before the twentieth century and became the national anthem only in 1931. But years earlier the Liberty Bell had been cherished in poem, song, and story and became the nation's most familiar symbol of patriotism.

Though the Liberty Bell cannot rival in size such bells as those at Saint Ivan's Church in Moscow (weighing sixty tons) or an ancient bell in Beijing (topping fifty-three tons), perhaps no bell in the world has ever played a greater historic role than the cracked bell. Though voiceless, it has been heard metaphorically everywhere in the world where people yearn for freedom. In our lifetime, it has acquired international star power with wattage great enough to become a global diplomatic asset.

If you go to the Liberty Bell Center in Philadelphia at

Sixth and Market streets, a block north of Independence Hall, you will find these words on the wall of the sparkling new building that is the Liberty Bell's third Philadelphia home: "Why do people from around the world choose to visit the Liberty Bell? Why does this now silenced bell resonate so directly with visitors from so many varied cultures? Perhaps the greatest strength of the Liberty Bell is the way it symbolizes the never-ending quest for freedom and the need to remain forever vigilant, for liberties gained can also be lost. This is the enduring message that the Liberty Bell embodies for all Americans and for our fellow citizens of the world."[1]

What, precisely, is this "enduring message"? It was inscribed on the bell at the direction of grave men more than two and a half centuries ago—legislators of the colony that the Quaker William Penn had founded in 1682. They had commissioned the bell to be cast in London and brought to North America to hang in the State House of the colony of Pennsylvania, and they had ordered very precisely that these prophetic words from the Old Testament be cast on the bell: "Proclaim Liberty throughout all the Land unto all the Inhabitants thereof."

Little did Pennsylvania's legislators know that these words from Leviticus would be the watchwords of generations to follow, in the United States and everywhere else in the world.

As the following pages explain, the Liberty Bell, once firmly fixed in the American mind as an avatar of all they believed their nation to be, was sent to and fro from Philadelphia across the continent. On the last of its seven trips, to San Francisco in 1915, in the midst of a world set afire by World War I, a journalist in San Diego opined that "there is not a single person in any state of the union who does not feel a personal interest in the bell." The historian of the Panama-Pacific Exposition echoed this: "The Bell is the great American patriotic symbol, almost a national Palladium. About that 20-odd hundred-weight of cracked metal there probably clings more of devotional feeling than about any other merely physical thing in the country. . . . Such is the grip of the concrete on the human mind. The abstract and the general are hard to grasp, and most people are willing, at least once in a while, to take the symbol for the substance."[2]

This was as true of Americans as any other people. *Amor patraie* is universal. Nurturing love of country relies heavily on symbols and relics of the past. That is how the Liberty Bell came to achieve iconic status.

The old Liberty Bell, crack and all, has borne the scars of history with dignity. Aside from the parchment on which the Declaration of Independence is written, it is the key artifact that links us to the struggle for freedom during the American Revolution. Ever since, it has been the inspiration for patriotic sacrifice in times of war and national crisis, though that was not uniformly the case: African Americans and women, for a long time, understood that the Liberty Bell did not ring for them. But it was second-class citizenship that gave the Liberty Bell another face. Going back to the 1830s, when the nation was becoming riven by the sectional crisis over slavery, the bell acquired another life as a tug-on-the-heart symbol for those who struggled for the unalienable rights guaranteed in the Declaration of Independence. For many years, it stood as a symbol of liberties gained by white male Americans; then, before long, it was appropriated as a reminder of liberties denied to many others. Ringing for everyone was the Liberty Bell's destiny. This is the message you will hear if you visit the Liberty Bell Center in Philadelphia today.

ONE

Beginnings

For almost seventy years an inconspicuous bell hanging from a branch in a tree behind colonial Pennsylvania's State House in Philadelphia was enough to summon the legislative assembly, announce the reading of public proclamations, ring in the new year, and warn of danger. William Penn, Quaker leader and Pennsylvania's founder, was said to have brought the bell himself to his City of Brotherly Love. But by 1751, after a decade of prosperity and heavy immigration of Germans and Scots-Irish, the city's authorities wanted a bell whose peal would have greater carrying power—"a distance-conquering bell," as one historian has put it—and toll with a resonance more dignified than the small bell that had heretofore sufficed. Philadelphia's population had already reached some fourteen thousand, and its ships plied the waters everywhere in the Atlantic basin. Philadelphia and its official bell were coming of age.[1]

The driving force behind the push for a notable bell was Isaac Norris II, the speaker of the Pennsylvania legislative assembly, the most democratic lawmaking body in the English colonies. Like his father, William Penn's trusted friend, Norris was admired as a successful merchant, and he was an adroit politician in the Quaker-dominated assembly as well as a pillar of the Society of Friends, who had kept peace between colonists and Indians for three generations. By 1743 he had retired from the countinghouse to devote himself to public affairs. Six years later, he had supervised the raising of an eye-catching tower on the south side of the State House to replace a modest bell cupola. This was part of the plan to allow Philadelphia, the capital to a thriving colony, to present itself to the world with architectural distinction. In 1751 Norris took the next step, writing to Robert Charles, Pennsylvania's agent in London, "to get us a good bell of about two thousand pounds weight." A bell of this size did not compare with "Great Tom," the five-ton bell that rang out from Saint Paul's Cathedral in London; yet it was larger by far than any other bell on the North American continent.

Then Norris sent precise orders that at the time might

not have seemed unusual but in the decades ahead would gain greater and greater power, like a snowball gaining mass on its way down a steep slope. Let the bell be inscribed, wrote Norris, with "well shaped large letters" around its waist that said: "Proclaim Liberty thro' all the Land to all the Inhabitants Thereof."

These words from the Bible—Leviticus, twenty-fifth chapter, tenth verse—were freighted with social and political meaning. These were words that would take on new layers of significance in different eras, in different contexts, and in different parts of the world. Little did the bell's commissioners know what lay ahead for this biblical verse. Certainly, they had no inkling that the bell's pealings would echo down the centuries and take on a world-encircling power to affect the modern age.

Why had Norris, with the assembly's consent, chosen words from an Old Testament verse? What effect did they hope such an inscription would have? The surviving sources do not speak clearly to us about this. But something is known, and much can be surmised. Norris had studied for two years in England and knew Hebrew, Latin, and French; he was also an avid student of the Bible. While a shrewd merchant, he was also a man trying to help Penn's colony navigate a period during which Quakers had lost their majority in the colony and were losing their grasp on the provincial legislature, which they had controlled since Quakers had arrived on the shores of the Delaware River three-quarters of a century before. Like many other Quakers, Norris was disillusioned with the sons of William Penn, now the colony's proprietors, who had turned from Quakerism to Anglicanism and were more interested in real estate profits than lofty ideals.

In consulting ancient texts, uppermost in Norris's mind was the assurance of Pennsylvania's bright future as a tolerant, fair-minded gathering of peoples from many parts of Europe and Africa. Inscribed on this great bell should be words to inspire, words to hold people to founding principles. Each clap of the bell would remind people of the social and political vision that Penn had called his "Holy Experiment."

What was in the minds of Isaac Norris and the legislative body that he led is abundantly clear in the inscription on the bell—"Proclaim Liberty throughout all the Land unto all the Inhabitants thereof": they prized liberty and thought of it as a universal right. But exactly what liberties? The biblical words surrounding the "proclaim liberty" clause shed light on this. The words in Leviticus preceding the bell's inscription are "And ye shall hallow the fiftieth year"; after it the verse continues: "it shall be a jubilee unto you; and ye shall return every man unto his possession, and ye shall return every man unto his family."

These words referred to the Israelites' Year of the Jubilee, an observance each half-century "in which property was redistributed, slaves freed, debts cancelled, and inequalities of the past fifty years removed."[2] This tradition resonated with the social and political situation in Pennsylvania in 1751. It had been exactly fifty years since William Penn, returning to England, granted a new frame of government, called the Frame of 1701, that created a unicameral legislature—the only one in British America—and gave it extensive new powers, broader powers than any other colonial legislature. Under pressure, Penn also made concessions in his feudal-like proprietary land system, where he received quitrents on all the property he sold to settlers, and he acquiesced to weakening his control over land disputes.

As for returning "every man unto his possession, and … every man unto his family," Norris and his fellow Quakers were keenly aware that John Woolman and Anthony Benezet, two maverick Quaker reformers, were railing against slavery in the "Holy Experiment" and calling on Quakers to cleanse themselves of their deep-dyed sin. In the year before Norris called for the bell with the "proclaim liberty" inscription, Benezet began teaching black students, most of them slaves, at his home in the evening and speaking of their capabilities. At the same time, Woolman, who had traveled extensively in the slave

South in the late 1740s, was composing his hard-hitting *cri de conscience* pamphlet, which he implored the Quakers to publish two years later as *Considerations on the Keeping of Negroes.* Though Norris and other Quaker legislators were slaveholders themselves and not yet ready to divest themselves of their slaves, the inscription that proclaimed liberty throughout the land to *all* the inhabitants thereof contained a strong, if muffled, antislavery message. Many years later, as we will see, abolitionists seized on these words on the bell in their own crusade to end slavery in America.

When Robert Charles received Isaac Norris's letter ordering a State House bell, he took the order to one of the oldest bell foundries in England. The Whitechapel Bell Foundry had been casting bells in London since 1570, and their metalworkers took great pride in their craft. A bell could last for centuries, and its sound—each bell had its own tone and temper—could imprint itself indelibly on those within its reach. Once a bell was cast and tested, the Whitechapel artisans carefully packed it for its long passage across the Atlantic. The great bell arrived in late August 1752 to a city buzzing with anticipation. After workmen brought it ashore and mounted it on a makeshift stand to test its sound, an unnamed Philadelphian sent the clapper flying to the side of the bell. The bell struck a loud bong, reverberated, and, to the horror of the crowd, cracked at the brim. "Our bell was generally liked & approved of," wrote Isaac Norris to his English correspondent, "but . . . I had the mortification to hear that it was cracked by the stroke of the clapper without any other violence as it was hung up to try the sound."[3] On its first stroke on the western edge of the Atlantic, the bell was rendered useless, now worth little more than scrap metal.

Perhaps the bell was weakened by the stormy, eleven-week Atlantic passage or by faulty packaging. Philadelphians believed that they were faultless. Most assuredly, it was not cracked, as later patriots would have it, because "the tones learned in Britain could not be repeated in the land prepared for Democracy."[4] Aghast at what had happened, Norris lost no time in dispatching a letter to Whitechapel Foundry. "Our judges," he wrote, "have generally agreed that [the bell's metal] was too high and brittle." But Whitechapel today, still in business in its fifth century, maintains that the bell was damaged in transit or was the victim of an inexperienced bell ringer, who incorrectly sent the clapper careening against the bell's brim. As late as 1972 Whitechapel Foundry insisted that the Pennsylvania State House bell was the only one in more than four centuries that had cracked in testing.[5]

What was to be done after paying Whitechapel Foundry 120 pounds—almost $8,000 in today's purchasing

"Coping the Bell," at Whitechapel Bell Foundry, c. 1850. Artisans lowered the cope over the bell to fix its shape. *A History of Bells and Description of Their Manufacture, as Practised at the Bell Foundry, Whitechapel* (London: Cassell, Petter, and Galpin, 1870)

power—for the bell? An attempt to repair it failed. Then Philadelphia brass founders John Pass and John Stow offered to recast the bell. At first this seemed ludicrous. Stow was only four years out of his training as a brass founder, and nobody in the English colonies had ever attempted casting a bell of this size. John Pass, a native of Malta, was probably trained there on an island where casting bells went back several centuries. His background is still shrouded in the mists of the past. However, it is known that Pass, before coming to Philadelphia, had owned Mount Holly Iron Furnace in New Jersey, so he must have been Stow's senior. Perhaps the two artisans had confidence that they could do better than the Whitechapel foundrymen because Philadelphia had already become the seaboard site of North America's most talented craftsmen. Nothing seemed too daunting in a city where Benjamin Franklin had provided an example of a leather-apron man, as artisans were called, rising from the bottom to achieve success and independence. Franklin's junto of ordinary artisans, gathering to improve themselves through reading and discussion, instilled in the city's artisans a can-do attitude. Stow was a charter member of the Union Library Company, where book reading probably increased his self-confidence.

Off to Stow's foundry on Second Street at the "Sign of the Three Bells" the cracked bell was carted. After creating a mold from it, Pass and Stow sledgehammered the Whitechapel bell to foundry floor rubble. Into the furnace went pieces small enough to melt down. Determining that insufficient copper had been used by the venerable London foundry—an astoundingly arrogant conclusion to come from a still immature provincial seaport—Pass and Stow added an ounce and a half of copper for each pound of the melted-down bell. On March 10, 1753, Isaac Norris wrote the London agent that "they have this day opened the mould, and have got a good bell, which I confess pleases me very much that we should first venture upon and succeed in the greatest bell cast, for ought I know, in English America."[6] Flushed with pride, Norris reported that the mold's letters, spelling out the Leviticus cry for freedom, were "I am told, better than in the old one." To judge by this, Philadelphia's unheralded brass founders—one of them who could not even sign his name—had outperformed the master artisans of London's venerable Whitechapel Foundry.

But how would the bell sound? A handsomely wrought bell was one thing; a fine-sounding bell was another. A bell of this quality was expected to have five musical tones which must be attuned to one another to create a harmonious sound. The ever-watchful Norris, writing to a Quaker friend, explained that "when thou comes down, thou may hear the sound and judge for thyself" and explained how the legislative assembly had decided on an extraordinarily democratic way to decide the worth of the bell: "People seem divided about the goodness or badness [of the bell]," so it was hung in a framework "in order that everybody may hear and judge—that is everybody who has any vote—whether it shall remain or be recast."[7] Since a majority of adult males in Philadelphia had enough property to qualify for the suffrage, the bell's fate lay in the hands of the broadly based citizenry.

The crowd that gathered was no doubt large because

the city's fathers provided a feast of beef, ham, cheese, po-
tatoes, bread, rum punch, and beer for the gala assemblage. But if the beer and beef were good, the bell was
not. The hoped-for melodious sound that everyone an-
ticipated instead registered as a discouraging thud, like
two coal scuttles banged against each other, as one witness put it. Teased by the crowd, Pass and Stow retreated
to their foundry to work at breakneck speed to recast the
bell a second time.[8]

The new bell—the third State House bell—was ready
by June 1753. The metallurgical knowledge of the time
was not sufficient to warn that such a melting down and
recasting would sap the resilience of the bell and leave
it more vulnerable to cracking. Nonetheless, this time
the bell passed muster, though not without objections.
"Though some are of the opinion that it will do," wrote
Isaac Norris, "I own I do not like it." Carpenters spent
four days raising the bell—which weighed in at just over
one ton, 2,080 pounds to be exact, and was about four feet
in diameter at the mouth—by stages into the steeple,
where it was hung from a yoke fashioned from American
elm in June 1753. Still hoping for something better, the
assembly asked Whitechapel Foundry to cast another
bell and accept their first bell for credit. It arrived in
spring 1754, just as frontier conflict erupted several hundred miles west of Philadelphia, soon to surge into the

French and Indian War. But Philadelphians preferred their locally cast bell, so it remained in the tower. There it hung, "The Old One," as it was later called, to announce the opening and adjournment of assembly sessions and other notable events. The second Whitechapel bell, which workmen wrestled to the dock after it arrived on May 3, 1754, was hoisted into the front of the tower. Five years later, it was attached to a new State House clock, proudly produced by a Philadelphia watchmaker, to toll the hours.[9] The biggest bell in North America now hung in the grandest public building in all of the British New World colonies.

Once hung, the Pass and Stow bell accumulated many responsibilities. First ringing out on August 27, 1753, to reconvene the legislative assembly, the Old Bell held to its main use for many years: to summon Pennsylvania colonial legislators to the State House to do the people's business. Not to take his seat within thirty minutes of the last clang of the bell cost a legislator one shilling. Combating tardy arrival and absenteeism, the assembly raised the penalty to two shillings and eight pence in 1762 and two shillings eighteen pence in 1764.[10] But it had other work to do. The bell rang for the accession of George III to the English throne on February 21, 1761, and it pealed again two years later to proclaim the end of the French and Indian War. These pealings announced good news;

but others soon followed that cut in a different direction. The bell rang out on October 26, 1764, as Benjamin Franklin departed for London to represent the colony as its agent at a time when the Sugar Act had raised protests and sent up storm signals of a rupture between the thirteen colonies and the mother country.

A year later, after Parliament had passed the Stamp Act, the bell became an accomplice in revolutionary politics. It convened the colony's legislative assembly in September 1765, as custom dictated. That led to heated debate in a city enveloped with tension, and soon an angry crowd threatened to pull down Franklin's house for his role in getting his friend, John Hughes, appointed as the royal stamp distributor. The assembly voted to send a strong protest to Parliament. But that was tame compared with the events of October 5, the day an English ship sailed up the Delaware River to deliver the stamped paper for implementing the Stamp Act. The Old Bell, along with the Christ Church bells, rang out to warn of the approaching ship. But this time the bell was shrouded so that the sharp, clear sound was replaced by a dolorous muffled peal. Gathering to the sound of the bell, Philadelphians flocked to the State House yard. John Hughes himself recorded the event: "A large number of people was raised and assembled at the state-house, where it was publicly declared . . . that if I did not immediately resign my office, my house should be pulled down and my sub-stance destroyed."[11]

For the next decade, the Old Bell tolled recurrently, marking the road to revolution. Little of the clanging promised sunny times. In April 1768 the bell drew thou-sands to protest the Townshend Duties. A few months later, on July 30, the bell again summoned Philadelphians to "consider instructions to our representatives in the present critical condition of these Colonies." Again, the bell pealed in September 1770 to summon Philadelphians to protest British policies diminishing their liberties. Next it rang to organize a boycott against imported En-glish goods. Once more, in February 1771, the bell con-vened a special session of the legislature to discuss colo-nial outrage over the perceived abusive policies of the British government.[12]

By 1772 some conservative Philadelphians had tired of the petitions, protests, remonstrations, and unruly gath-erings in the State House yard initiated by the clanging of the Old Bell. For them, the bell was ringing out treason or leading toward it. Gathering themselves, they petitioned the assembly to silence the bell. "The too frequent ring-ing by the great bell in the steeple of the State House," read the petition, "has often been felt severely when some of the petitioners' families have been affected with sick-ness, at which times, from its uncommon size and unusual sound, it is extremely dangerous and may prove fatal." It is possible that the petitioners were complaining only about their ears ringing too much. But the remainder of their petition indicates that the Old Bell's use as a tocsin to press the agenda of radical revolutionaries was uppermost in their minds. "The petitioners conceive that [the bell] was never designed to be rung on any other than public occasions, such as the times of meeting of the honorable assembly of the province, and of the courts of justice."[13]

But the ringing went on: to assemble the citizenry in October 1773 for a town meeting to protest the Tea Act; two months later to protest the arrival of a tea-laden English ship; twice in June 1774 to protest the Coercive Acts that closed the port of Boston; and, most memorably, to hurry some eight thousand Philadelphians to the State House to hear the portentous news in April 1775—brought by Paul Revere after a five-day dash on his magnificent mare, Brown Betty, from Boston to the Quaker city—about the firefights at Lexington and Concord. Less than a month later, from its lofty perch in the steeple, the Old Bell rung out to announce the convening of the Second Continental Congress at the State House, and on June 16 it tolled the appointment of George Washington as general of the Continental Army.[14]

In late May 1776 the bell played its part to break the

stalemate in the Continental Congress as it debated taking the plunge by declaring independence. The delegates from Pennsylvania, soon to be called the Keystone State, refused to endorse the call for independence led by Massachusetts and Virginia delegates. So Philadelphia "independents," led by Thomas Paine and his friends, called for a mass meeting "to take the sense of the people respecting the resolve of Congress." With the Old Bell ringing on the rainy morning of May 20, Philadelphians swarmed to the State House yard. There they shouted approval for a resolution declaring that the instructions from Pennsylvania's legislature to its delegates not to vote for independence "have a dangerous tendency to withdraw this province from that happy union with the other colonies." The legislature surrendered to the will of Philadelphia's people, and the logjam was broken. It was not yet the Liberty Bell, still just the State House Bell. But it did its part in moving the colonies toward the "leap into the dark" that would make the bell iconic.

The moment that enshrined the Old Bell came six weeks later. After two days of solemn debate, the Continental Congress adopted the Declaration of Independence on July 4 and ordered it printed. Newspapers rolled the Declaration off their presses on July 6. Two more days elapsed before its first public reading. Dawn ushered in a "warm, sunshine morning" on July 8, 1776, and the Old

Pennsylvania State House in Philadelphia. Note the huge clock on the
side of the building, which still stands today. Courtesy Independence
National Historical Park

Bell began to peal around 11 A.M. With people massed in
the State House yard, Colonel John Nixon, son of an
Irish immigrant, read the Declaration of Independence at
high noon. Three huzzahs followed the reading, and then
the bell began to clang, part of a chorus of church bells
pealing throughout the city. It was the moment for which
the bell would become forever famous. Christopher Marshall, a Quaker pharmacist, recorded in his diary that the
celebrating continued through the afternoon and into the
night. "There were bonfires, ringing bells, with other great
demonstrations of joy upon the unanimity and agreement

William Birch, State House, Philadelphia, 1799. The deteriorating
steeple had been removed and the State House bell lowered to a
louvered floor of the tower by the time of Birch's painting.
Visiting Native Americans tented by the State House.
Courtesy Library Company of Philadelphia

of the Declaration." John Adams wrote that "the bells
rang all day and almost all night."[15]

Only one year elapsed before the tradition arose in
Philadelphia of ringing bells on July Fourth, not July
Eighth, as the birthday of the United States. On July 4,
1777, speeches were accompanied by bell ringing and
cannon firing, climaxing in the evening with fireworks.
But soon the celebrations turned to consternation as the
British army bore down on Philadelphia.

The British occupation of Philadelphia in September

1777, capping a series of blows to the "Glorious Cause," as the Patriots called their struggle for independence, drove thousands of Pennsylvanians from their capital city. Going with them was anything of use to the British occupying army—horses, blankets, lead pipes, foodstuffs, and bells. Twelve days before the British army marched into the city—the battle at Brandywine was already in progress—Philadelphia's many churches took down their bells, knowing that the British would melt and recast them into cannon balls and musket shot. The Old Bell itself would have provided some thirty thousand rounds of ammunition. Lowering the bell from the State House steeple, carpenters loaded it on a heavy wagon, which then made its way north and west to the small German-dominated town of Bethlehem in company of a seven hundred–wagon train with a military escort of some two hundred cavalrymen from North Carolina and Virginia. From there, wagoners carted the bell another thirteen miles to Allentown. There patriots hid the one-ton bell beneath the floor of the Zion German Reformed Church. Like a high-value diplomat secreted behind false paneling in a small embassy room, the Old Bell waited out the British occupation of Philadelphia.

When the British decamped in June 1778, pursued by Washington's Continental Army, which had been en-camped at Valley Forge for six months, Philadelphians flocked back to their city much abused by the occupying army. The Old Bell came back as well. But for now it had lost its voice because the fine steeple had rotted badly and could not in this condition support the yoke from which the bell had hung. So the bell was stored at the tower's brick enclosed midlevel to await a better day.[16] Hemmed in by louvers that diminished its reach, the Old Bell sedately announced the British surrender at Yorktown on October 24, 1781. At the legislative assembly's order, "four pieces of artillery responded to the pealing of the bell, and all the city bells answered." Shortly thereafter, General Washington and his wife returned triumphantly to Philadelphia to the pealing of the Old Bell. It tolled again on April 15, 1783, to announce the signing of the Treaty of Paris with Great Britain that finally brought the long war to an end.[17]

Though this was a glorious end of an eight-year war to celebrate, the bell's glory days were also coming to an end. The Constitutional Convention that convened in Philadelphia in May 1787 was an occasion for the bell to ring, and the Old Bell tolled the opening of state legislative sessions. But by 1799, after it rang to mourn the death of George Washington, the bell lost much of its voice. When Pennsylvania's state capital moved inland to

Lancaster (and thirteen years later to Harrisburg) and the national capital moved to Washington, D.C., a year later, Philadelphia was no longer the political nerve center for state and national politics. The State House and its venerable bell were abruptly stripped of their chief function. Within a few years, the Old Bell looked down on a place of "vice and indecorum," as the city council characterized the neighborhood around the State House.[18]

The State House gained a new lease on life in 1801 when Charles Willson Peale, the city's prolific portrait painter and creator of public art, leased for his growing natural history museum the second floor and east assembly room of the first floor, where the Declaration of Independence and Constitution had been written, debated, and signed. Museumgoers flocked to see Peale's life-sized wax figures of a Sandwich Islander, a "Sooty African," a Chinese laborer, and several American Indians; stuffed birds, enormous rattlesnakes, and other wild beasts; and a three-foot Madagascar bat and an anteater measuring more than seven feet from snout to tail. Those who cared to climb the stairs into what was left of the decaying tower could see the seldom-rung Old Bell sharing space with Peale's marine specimens, including scores of mounted fish, amphibians, and three hundred–pound Indian Ocean oyster shells.

By 1812, in Philadelphia's first burst of urban renewal,

the Old Bell almost became an orphan. Obtaining permission from the state to replace the piazzas and wing buildings of the State House, the city erected offices in row house style. With its steeple long gone and its pleasing triadic arrangement now discarded, the State House only partially resembled the building where the nation's birth had occurred. The Old Bell, meanwhile, narrowly escaped a brush with death. Eyeing the rotting hulk of the State House and scraping for funds to build the new state capitol building on the Susquehanna River, Pennsylvania's legislature proposed to demolish the State House altogether and sell the property to developers. Even the Old Bell seemed nothing more than a rusty, less-than-perfect chimer. As a later preservationist commented ruefully, the bell was not thought worth mentioning in the plan to raze the State House "but left to be sold" along with the "old lumber within the walls and rafters of Independence Hall."[19] Much the same had been done a few years before in erecting row houses a few blocks away on the site of Benjamin Franklin's house, which had been demolished after his family sold it to developers.

The city of Philadelphia resisted, but state legislators proposed the demolitions again in 1816. Patriotic attachment to the site of the nation's birth figured little in the legislature's planning because the public itself was indifferent to preserving what would later become a national icon. Obliterating venerable buildings was for many Americans a means of freeing themselves from the tyranny of forerunners—what Henry David Thoreau called a "purifying destruction."

Just when it seemed that the State House and the Old Bell were about to be sacrificed to urban renewal, William Duane, the Jeffersonian publisher of the newspaper founded by Benjamin Franklin Bache, Franklin's grandson, rallied Philadelphians in 1816. "In Pennsylvania, under the Gothic mist of ignorance and vice, by which it is now governed," he wrote, "everything is to be pulled down." The structure where the Declaration of Independence "was deliberated and determined," he thundered, should be venerated "as a monument of that splendid event, but this is not the spirit of the rulers of Pennsylvania now—the state house must be sold—for everything now in political affairs is barter and sale!"[20] Goaded by Duane, the city brokered a deal under which $70,000 paid to the state would make Philadelphia forever the owner of the State House, the Old Bell, and the State House yard. Though in recent years it had rung out only on special occasions, the bell was now at least safe.

Eight years later, when the marquis de Lafayette made his triumphal, thirteen-month tour through the United States in 1824–25, the bell began to acquire a new life, largely through the publicity paid to the crumbling State

House. A hero on both sides of the Atlantic for his roles in the American and French revolutions, Lafayette journeyed to every corner of the country. Beginning to understand that while history is about the past, it is for the future, Philadelphians began preparing for Lafayette's visit. City officials chose the east room of the State House as the proper place to receive the marquis, and this obliged them to restore the now shabby chamber. The refurnished room, featuring mahogany sofas and luxurious draperies and carpets in red and blue, far outshone the chamber where the delegates to the Continental Congress had signed the Declaration of Independence a half-century before. The east room instantly became a hallowed space after Lafayette sent chills down the spines of all those attending by reminding them that "here within these sacred walls, . . . was boldly declared the independence of these United States. Here, sir, was planned the formation of our virtuous, brave revolutionary army and the providential inspiration received that gave the command of it to our beloved, matchless Washington."[21] Philadelphians went wild. For seven days they paraded, celebrated, raised monuments, held grand receptions, and poured out their adoration. Entrepreneurs scrambled to put Lafayette's image on whatever had commercial value—cravats, brandy flasks, white kid gloves, snuffboxes, glasses, pitchers, gewgaws, and linen handkerchiefs.

From this point on, the "State House" became "Independence Hall." The Old Bell would have to wait another decade to find its identity, but at least it would ascend to a higher perch. Four years after Lafayette's memorable visit, the municipal government ordered the rebuilding of the wooden steeple that had been demolished forty-five years before. The new steeple occasioned debate. Should it replicate the old steeple where the Old Bell had rung out? That would preserve historical memory by reviving a precious artifact of the revolutionary era. Or should Philadelphia look to the future with a new design from the hands of the architects who were already transforming the city? For a city already being called the Athens of America for its architects and artists, this would reflect Philadelphia's unsentimental, dynamic culture.

Leading the new way forward was William Strickland, an architect and engineer who had refurbished the State House in 1824 and designed the Greek Revival Second Bank of the United States. Charged with drawing up plans for a new State House superstructure, he designed a new tower rising about thirty feet higher in brick with a cupola and spire atop it. But city councilors, eager to restore the tower and steeple "to the state in which it stood in 1776," objected strenuously, urging that this "sacred spot—a sacred building" be restored to its form of a half-century previous. Strickland complied. By July 4, 1828, the new steeple, mimicking the 1776 version, was complete. Even while urban renewal had erased important parts of the State House neighborhood, the rebuilding of Independence Hall initiated an era of historic restoration that soon would encompass Washington's Mount Vernon and other revolutionary-era sites.[22]

But what about the Old Bell? In a city that had grown spectacularly since Washington's death in 1799, from 35,000 to 150,000, Philadelphia dearly needed a fire watchtower, for it had been ravaged by numerous blazes in its densely populated neighborhoods, where warrens of new immigrants huddled. Also needed was a new reliable clock and bell to monitor the new rhythms of an industrializing city, where clock time was replacing sidereal time. Keeping abreast of the changing times, the city councils commissioned a new bell and a four-faced clock, illuminated at night, to be installed in the cupola. Constructed by a Philadelphia craftsman, William Meredith, the new bell took on an important responsibility—as a fire alarm, from which Philadelphians would learn that one stroke meant a fire to the north of Independence Hall, two strokes to the south, three peals to the east, and four to the west. Meanwhile, the Old Bell remained suspended in the fourth floor of the brick part of the tower. William Meredith, the new bellmaker, was asked to cart away the Old Bell as scrap metal; but the cost of lowering it with blocks and tackle and hauling it to the foundry was not deemed to be worth the $400 the city fathers wanted for it.[23] So Meredith refused the bell, and only this saved it.

There, below the steeple, the Old Bell rested for many years, apparently pealing only occasionally. It pealed for "Year of Jubilee," the fiftieth anniversary of the Declaration of Independence on July 4, 1826. Twenty days later, muffled for the sorrowful occasion, it tolled to observe the death of Thomas Jefferson and John Adams.[24] Honoring another hero of the American Revolution, it tolled on the day that news arrived of Lafayette's death in 1834. But the bell was not yet revered or even particularly protected. William Linn, looking back from the early twentieth century to his boyhood, remembered that "we would go down to the old Bell and, with paving stones, try to knock off a piece of it. . . . If the Bell would break at all, it would have broken then, when these boys hammered it with pieces of iron and stones trying to get a piece off."[25] This was only the beginning of relic hunters trying to break off pieces of the Liberty Bell; some planned to recast them into miniature replicas.

With the Old Bell now at rest, the city had to find a home for the other Liberty Bell—the Whitechapel bell. In a gesture of conciliation in a city now filling with tension between Protestants and Catholics, the municipal government gave the second Whitechapel bell to Saint

Augustine Roman Catholic Church on Fourth Street below Vine in 1828. There it announced church services for sixteen years until it fell victim to raging tensions between Protestants and Catholics in what had become a city of anything but brotherly love. A crazed Protestant mob, filled with venom against Irish Catholic immigrants, attacked Saint Augustine's in the summer of 1844 and burned it to the ground. From what remained of the bell, a new bell was recast. It rests peacefully today inside the campus library of Villanova University.[26]

While the restoration of what was now being called Independence Hall put a stamp on the building as a sacred place, connecting the past with the present, the Old Bell still awaited its awakening from a long slumber. By the 1830s the metropolis was a destination for scores of visitors, including Charles Dickens and Alexis de Tocqueville. But far from hurrying to Independence Hall, they wanted to see the new Eastern State Penitentiary, a massive granite fortress where every prisoner was kept in strict solitary confinement—an experiment in teaching convicts to be penitent and thus eventually reclaim themselves as useful members of society. Those who were interested in Independence Hall could enter its doors only by calling a janitor to open the "Hall of Independence" with a key. Most visitors hurried past the place where the nation's sacred documents had been signed, eager to ascend the new steeple where they could gaze out at the burgeoning city from ninety-five feet, the highest viewpoint available, with the new clock bell twenty-three feet above them. Looking down on Chestnut Street, one visitor viewed "the care-worn merchant at his bales, the laborer at his toil, the rich man's coach . . . upon its gilded wheels."[27] If any noticed the Old Bell much lower in the tower, they left no comments on it at all in the late 1820s. But its time was coming.

TWO

The Bell Becomes an Icon

"Whoever shall write a history of Philadelphia from the [eighteen-] Thirties to the end of the Fifties will record a popular period of turbulence and outrages so extensive as to now appear almost incredible." Thus wrote Charles Godfrey Leland, a spirited Philadelphia journalist and poet who was looking back from the 1890s after a life of covering the city. The turbulence and outrages in the decades before the Civil War to which Leland referred were vicious racial and religious riots trammeling the city in an era before a municipal police force quelled them by collaring the street gangs—Moyamensing Killers, Scroungers, Whelps, Flayers, Stingers, Bouncers, Hyenas, Bedbugs, Swampoodle Terriers, Bloodtubs, Gumballs, Nighthawks, and Deathfetchers—that had terror-

31

ized the City of Brotherly Love. Yet it was in this same period that Philadelphians struck off reform societies like so many new coins and that the Liberty Bell acquired the name now known around the world. But before this happened, the bell developed the crack so familiar to today's visitors who, two million strong, pass by the American icon each year.

For many years, the story has been passed down that the Old Bell cracked—from the lip toward its crown—when it was tolling on July 8, 1835, as the funeral procession of John Marshall, the longest-serving chief justice of the Supreme Court, solemnly passed through the city. Marshall had died at the Walnut Street boardinghouse of a Mrs. Crim, and now the body was on the way to the docks, where a steamboat awaited to carry Marshall's remains back to Virginia. It's a touching story, giving the bell a heart and soul capable of expressing grief at the news of a great man's death. Yet no Philadelphia newspaper reported what surely would have been a newsworthy event. Still, *The Official Guide Book to Philadelphia: A New Handbook for Strangers and Visitors*, published in 1875 for the Centennial Exposition in Philadelphia, made this claim authoritatively, and many popular pamphlets and books have followed suit. In 1935, the hundredth anniversary of Marshall's death, the *New York Times* and other metro newspapers gave front-page attention to the cracking of the bell at the Marshall cortège. As late as the mid-twentieth century, schoolchildren learned this story of the heartbroken bell.[1]

But this is one of many stories. In other accounts, each soaked with emotion, the bell cracked on different dates and occasions. According to one tale, the bell cracked in May 1829 while ringing in the news of Great Britain's Catholic Relief Act, which gave Catholics a right to sit in Parliament (while disenfranchising most Irish Catholics by increasing fivefold the amount of property they needed to qualify as voters). Seventy years later, John Sartain, a celebrated Philadelphia artist, reminisced that when he was up in the Independence Hall tower viewing the cracked bell two years after this event, he was told by the custodian of the building that "the bell refused to ring for a British Act, even when the Act was a good one."[2]

Other historical accounts, none substantiated by contemporary sources, insist that the Old Bell cracked on February 22, 1832, while pealing for the centennial of Washington's birthday. Another claimed it was on Washington's birthday three years later, and still another on his birthday in 1843. Most touching is the story published in the *New York Times* in 1911 under the headline "How I Broke the Liberty Bell—By the Boy Who Broke It." Emmanuel Joseph Rauch, then eighty-six years old, told the *Times* that as he passed by Independence Hall on Washington's birthday in 1835—at that time he was ten years old—the custodian of the steeple asked him whether he would like to ring the bell in remembrance of the *pater patraie*. Here was a boy's wildest dream! With other boys—"a squad of urchins"—gathered by the steeple keeper, the *Times* reported, Rauch was instructed how to pull the rope to set the bell ringing. But the bell's tone was peculiar, its voice distorted. When the bell keeper climbed up into the tower to examine the bell, he was aghast to find a foot-long crack. Told to go home, the boys sheepishly climbed back down from the steeple and fled.[3]

From this welter of stories, the most reputable account is that the bell cracked on Washington's birthday in 1843. This was claimed forty-six years later by Willis P. Hazard, who updated John Fanning Watson's *Annals of Philadelphia and Pennsylvania in the Olden Time*, Philadelphia's first history. Beyond question, Philadelphia's city government resolved that the bell should be rung on Washington's birthday in 1846, and to do this Independence Hall's superintendent arranged to smooth out the two sides of the crack in the bell so that the jagged sides would not vibrate against each other. This, it was thought, would improve the Old Bell's tone and prevent further fracturing. Philadelphia's *Public Ledger* published an account of the

sad result of this in 1846 under the headline "The Old Independence Bell." Having been put in good order—or so
it was thought—the bell began pealing in the morning.
"It gave out clear notes and loud, and appeared to be in
excellent condition until noon, when it received a sort of
compound fracture in a zig-zag direction through one of
its sides, which put it completely out of tune and left it a
mere wreck of what it was." The *Ledger* writer, thinking
he was writing an obituary of the bell, wrote that "this
venerable relic of the revolution rang its last clear note on
Monday last, in honor of the birth day of Washington,
and now hangs in the great city steeple irreparably
cracked and forever dumb." Perhaps the bell should be
melted down and recast, opined the *Public Ledger* journalist, since "it is now entirely useless."[4] Little could he
imagine that a cracked bell would become iconic, crack
and all.

Even before the two fracturings in 1843 and 1846, the
bell had begun to acquire a new identity. Not Philadelphians but New Yorkers and Bostonians appropriated the
old State House bell as an emblem of the growing campaign to abolish slavery in the "land of the free and the
home of the brave." In the revolutionary era, Philadelphia had stood tall as the center of the first efforts to abolish slavery in a land where bondage had become the main-

stay of the South and a fixture of the North's maritime commerce. But Philadelphia had surrendered its primacy as a center of antislavery sentiment by the 1820s after David Walker's fiery pamphlet *Address to the Negro People* was published in Boston in 1829 and William Lloyd Garrison's equally fiery abolitionist newspaper, *The Liberator,* began to roll off the press there two years later. In 1835 the New York Anti-Slavery Society's *Anti-Slavery Record* named the old State House bell "The Liberty Bell" with biting language aimed at Philadelphians: "May not the emancipationists in Philadelphia hope to live to hear the same bell rung, when liberty shall in fact be proclaimed to all the inhabitants of this favored land? Hitherto, the bell has not obeyed the inscription; and its peals have been a mockery, while one sixth of 'all inhabitants' are in abject slavery."[5] Just as Josiah Wedgwood's ceramic medallion depicting a kneeling slave in chains asking "Am I Not a Man and a Brother?" became a totem of the transatlantic antislavery movement, the old State House bell's inscription "Proclaim Liberty throughout all the Land" made it fitting that the one-ton chimer should be rechristened as the Liberty Bell. Two years later, the New York Anti-Slavery Society's publication titled *Liberty* displayed a stylized version of the State House bell as its frontispiece, with the words "Proclaim Freedom."

Philadelphians had not abandoned the abolitionist crusade, which had entered its radical phase, where moral suasion was seen as ineffective and confrontational tactics were gaining force. But nobody in the Quaker city followed the New Yorkers' lead in linking the State House bell to the struggle to cleanse American society from its scourge. This timidity probably owes something to the burning of Pennsylvania Hall, erected as a place for anti-slavery advocates to assemble and speechify, two days after it opened in May 1838. With the constables standing by, a pro-slavery mob, especially infuriated by the abolitionists' biracial meetings, stoned the windows while the Anti-Slavery Convention of American Women met inside, then returned the following night to burn the hall to the ground. Philadelphia abolitionists persevered, but with most of the city against them, they remained on the defensive for the next several decades.

Bostonian abolitionists were less intimidated, though pro-slavery sentiment in the Massachusetts capital was rife. Nonetheless, antislavery leaders soon followed the New Yorkers' use of the Liberty Bell. Boston's Friends of Liberty began displaying Philadelphia's Old Bell in 1839 in its publication now titled *The Liberty Bell*. Sold at their annual Anti-Slavery Fair, their pamphlets often included poems to the Philadelphia "Liberty Bell" ringing out

American freedom and, it was hoped, soon the emancipation of enslaved Americans (nearly three million of them by 1840). Garrison's *Liberator* published George Kent's poem "The Liberty Bell" in 1839, taking dead aim at the bell that did *not* proclaim liberty for all throughout the land:

> In shame this truth we own
> That palls upon the heart.
> All white men—they alone
> Have as boon a part
> In double sense! We palter
> We make of truth a lie
> Bow down at Freedom's altar
> In base hypocrisy.[6]

Where the kneeling slave with the caption "Am I Not a Man and a Brother?" had reigned for more than half a century as the abolitionists' most engaging image, now Philadelphia's Old Bell, christened the Liberty Bell, gained international recognition. Deploying the Liberty Bell to hold Americans to account, the Bostonian abolitionists became more and more strident in their calls for universal freedom. In 1833 Great Britain had ended slavery in its West Indies colonies while sectional tension grew in the United States as pro- and antislavery advocates hardened their positions. Mindful of this, Boston's Friends of Liberty filled their pamphlets with Liberty Bell allusions. By 1842 their *Liberty Bell* opened with a poem calling the bell "the tocsin of freedom and slavery's knell" and pleading that

Our Liberty Bell! Let its startling tone,
Abroad o'er a slavish land be thrown!

Another writer challenged Americans to stand by their founding principles: "The Liberty Bell is fixed on the world's watch tower . . . so will its cheering tones ever ring out amid Freedom's passes, until every chain shall be broken and one loud shout shall proclaim the glorious Jubilee of universal emancipation. Is it to be Tyrants amid Slaves that Americans, with Liberty glowing on every page of their history, and the glorious Declaration of Independence upon their lips, have been found willing to degrade themselves? Shame on you!"[7]

Bostonians kept up their drumbeat, invoking the Liberty Bell again and again in abolitionist literature. In 1845 subscribers of *The Liberty Bell* read that

Liberty's Bell hath sounded its bold peal
Where Man holds Man in Slavery! At the sound—
Ye who are faithful 'mid the faithless found,
Answer its summons with unfaltering zeal.

Four years later, "St. Denis" contributed a mournful re-
flection:

> Beyond the wild Atlantic wave,
> In Penn's fair city, calm and grave,
> Hangs the old bell which rings no more,
> For Freedom sleeps on Freedom's shore.[8]

Only a year after the bell suffered its irreparable crack
and fell silent, George Lippard, a dashing young journalist who wielded a pen dipped in crimson and whose voice
rang out in the violence-filled and immigrant-heavy city,
spun out a tale that turned the Old Bell into the Liberty
Bell forever. His story of how the State House bell announced the Declaration of Independence on July 4,
1776, and thus became the "Independence Bell" or the
"Liberty Bell" built on a growing identification of the
Old Bell as a symbol of liberty. One of Philadelphia's
most popular newspapers spoke of the bell in 1828 with
reverence, reminding readers that "it often pealed those
treasured tones that soon should tell when freedom's
proudest scroll was sealed."[9]

With the American public gradually becoming accustomed to thinking of the old Pass and Stow bell cast in
1753 as the Liberty Bell, Lippard, like many a shrewd
journalist, began to cash in. His story about the Liberty
Bell's epic moment was emotional, clever, and entirely

SONNET

SUGGESTED BY THE INSCRIPTION ON THE
PHILADELPHIA LIBERTY BELL.

It is no tocsin of affright we sound,
  Summoning nations to the conflict dire ; —
  No fearful peal from cities wrapped in fire
  Echoes, at our behest, the land around : —
  Yet would we rouse our country's utmost bound

Frontispiece of *The Liberty Bell* (1839)

fabricated. Lippard already had a mass following by the
early 1840s, when his *Quaker City; or, The Monks of Monk
Hall*—filled with exposés of sex, violence, terror, lust, and
exploitation in the once staid city of William Penn—sold

sixty thousand copies in its first year, more copies than Parson Weems's popular biography of George Washington had sold between 1800 and 1830. Having captured the public's attention, he turned to stories about the American Revolution. Restless, ambitious, and a radical friend of labor, Lippard churned out tales that freshened the public's memory of local battles that had been fought at Germantown and Brandywine before the British occupied the city in September 1777. These appeared in *Washington and His Generals; or, Legends of the American Revolution* in 1848.

With the public eating from his hand, Lippard concocted "The Fourth of July, 1776," the Liberty Bell story that would live on for generations as a genuine account of the glad tidings announced by the ringing of the bell on that first Independence Day. It was this story that gave the bell its fame. First published on January 2, 1847, in the *Saturday Courier*, a mass-circulation Philadelphia magazine, and then a year later in Lippard's *Washington and His Generals*, the tale recounted that the fifty-six Founding Fathers of the Second Continental Congress gathered to hear a stirring oration from "a tall slender man . . . dressed in a dark robe" who cudgeled the faint-hearted Congressmen to take the momentous leap into the dark. "They surged forward to sign the Declaration," wrote Lippard. "Look! How they rush forward—stout-hearted

John Hancock has scarcely time to sign his bold name, before the pen is grasped by another—another and another! Look how the names blaze on the Parchment, Adams and Lee and Jefferson and Carroll, and now Roger Sherman the Shoemaker." Meanwhile, an old bell ringer in the steeple waited for the signal.

Lippard's further description defies comparison for sheer bathos. To today's readers his prose may seem ridiculously purplish, yet it became one of the most resonant legends in American history. And it sealed the new name of the old State House bell as the Liberty Bell. Here is an abbreviated version of what Lippard told his audience:

> In yonder wooden steeple, which crowns the red
> brick State House, stands an old man with white
> hair and sunburnt face. He is clad in humble attire,
> yet his eye gleams, as it is fixed upon the ponderous
> outline of the bell, suspended in the steeple there.
> The old man tries to read the inscription on that
> bell, but cannot. . . . He scarcely can spell one
> of those strange words carved on the surface of
> that bell.
>
> By his side . . . stands a flaxen-haired boy, with
> laughing eyes of summer blue. "Come here, my
> boy; you are a rich man's child. You can read. Spell
> me those words, and I'll bless ye, my good child!"

PROCLAIM LIBERTY TO ALL THE LAND AND ALL THE
INHABITANTS THEREOF.

"Look here, my child? Wilt do the old man a
kindness? Then haste you downstairs, and wait in
the hall by the big door until a man shall give you a
message for me. . . . When he gives you that word,
then run out yonder in the street, and shout it up to
me. Do you mind?"

It needed no second command. The boy with
blue eyes and flaxen hair . . . threads his way down
the dark stairs. . . . The crowds gathered more
darkly along the pavement and over the lawn, yet
still the boy came not. "Ah!" groaned the old man,
"he has forgotten me! These old limbs will have to
totter down the State House stairs, and climb up
again." . . . As the word was on his lips, a merry,
ringing laugh broke on the ear. There, among the
crowds on the pavement, stood the blue-eyed boy,
clapping his tiny hands, while the breeze blew his
flaxen hair all about his face.

And then swelling his little chest, he raised himself on tip-toe and shouted a single word—"Ring!"

Do you see that old man's eye fire? Do you see
that arm so suddenly bared to the shoulder, do you
see that withered hand, grasping the Iron Tongue of

the Bell? The old man is young again; his veins are filled with new life. Backward and forward, with sturdy strokes, he swings the Tongue. The Bell speaks out! The crowd in the street hear it, and burst forth in one long shout! Old Delaware hears it, and gives it back in the hurrah of her thousand sailors. The city hears it, and starts up from the desk and workbench, as though an earthquake had spoken. . . . Boom—boom-boom—the Bell speaks to the city and the world.

In fact, the Declaration was first read at high noon on July 8, while a surging crowd ripped the King's Arms from the wall of the State House courtroom and cast it, as one witness put it, upon "a pile of casks erected upon the commons, for the purpose of a bonfire, . . . the arms placed on the top."[10] The signing of the parchment did not begin until August 2—only John Hancock and the Congress's secretary, Charles Thomson, signed on that day—and the last signer did not inscribe his name until January 18, 1777. And there was no illiterate old bell ringer or blue-eyed, flaxen-haired boy who gave the signal to ring the bell. It is possible that the bell did not ring at all because of the dangerously deteriorated condition of the steeple.

Nonetheless, Lippard's legend lived on. In 1848, the year after the concocted story thrilled the public, Benson

J. Lossing, a New York newspaper editor and wood en-
graver who devoted much of his life to saving and restoring the nation's most venerable historic sites, came to
Philadelphia to gather material for his *Pictorial Field-Book
of the Revolution*. Lossing was furious to see Carpenters'
Hall, the meeting place of the First Continental Congress, "consecrated by the holiest associations which clus-
ter around the birthtime of our republic," given no respect
from Philadelphians as an important historic site. Instead, it was being used as a slovenly auction house, which
seemed to bother nobody. "What a desecration!" sput-
tered Lossing. "Covering the facade of the very Temple
of Freedom with the placards of groveling mammon! If
sensibility is shocked with this outward pollution, it is
overwhelmed with indignant shame on entering the hall
where ... the godfathers of our republic convened to
stand as sponsors at the baptism of infant American Liberty, to find it filled with every species of merchandise.. . .
Is there not patriotism strong enough and bold enough in
Philadelphia to enter this temple and 'cast out all of them
that buy and sell, and overthrow the table of the money-
changers'?"[11]

Then Lossing visited Independence Hall and discov-
ered some satisfaction. The Philadelphians cherished Independence Hall, he found, "as the most revered relic of
the war for independence." Ascending to the steeple, Los-

Just before this decision, a Philadelphia newspaperman, George "Gaslight" Foster, had written that the bell, "having faithfully performed its mission, now hangs broken and useless, yet a sacred memento of days that have shed a halo upon the world's history"; he "felt our veneration very strongly excited" by the "rough and scarred" bell. A Philadelphia guidebook in 1852 called the bell a "hallowed relic of the past" and printed a poem equating the bell with American freedom.[13] But the bell was not much visited. And it was not the bell that tolled for everyone.

Freedom it was for many but not for all. In fact, slavery and freedom were joined at the hip in Independence Hall in the 1850s. On the first floor, in the Assembly Room, Philadelphia's dignitaries gave the exiled Hungarian freedom fighter Lajos Kossuth a lavish reception in December 1851. Two years later, in July 1853, Philadelphia's finest gave President Franklin Pierce and his cabinet, including Jefferson Davis, a ceremonious welcome as Mayor Sherman Gilpin proclaimed, "We have now no living actor and witness of that time when the ponderous bell, though mute now, spoke volumes then but still speaks volumes now—'Proclaim liberty throughout the land and to all the inhabitants thereof.'"[14] Upstairs, on the second floor, acting under the Fugitive Slave Act of 1850, federal judges were hearing testimony on alleged runaway slaves who had fled their owners and taken refuge in the City of Brotherly Love. The court sent those convicted south below the Mason-Dixon Line. Deploring this paradox, an African-American newspaper published in the nation's capital fulminated that the fugitive slave hearings "took place in INDEPENDENCE HALL . . . on the very spot where the immortal words, fresh from the pen of Jefferson, that 'all men are created free and equal; that they were endowed by their Creator with certain unalienable rights; that among these are life, *liberty*, and the pursuit of happiness'; were proclaimed to the world as the platform of universal man, and the basis of his eternal right to resist oppression."[15]

Philadelphia's swelling black population—about eleven thousand by 1850—did not stand by idly. As some of their own were hauled to Independence Hall, they did their best to see justice served. In autumn of 1851 the entire city trembled as thirty-three blacks and five whites were tried for treason for their role in the "Christiana riot," in which they had defended fugitives from Maryland who had reached Lancaster County west of the city. A white Maryland slaveowner, pursuing a runaway slave, was killed in the fracas, and the ensuing debate created national headlines. Pennsylvania abolitionists pleaded that "those colored men were only following the example of Washington and the American heroes of '76." But a white crowd outside Independence Hall urged swift judgment "to ferret out and punish the murderers thus guilty of the double crime of assaulting the Constitution, and of taking the lives of men in pursuit of their recognized and rightful property." On the trial's first day, blacks and whites alike, according to the *National Era*, "blocked up the passage-way through Independence Hall, leading to the Court-room." Then, when the doors to the chamber opened up, "the crowd rush[ed] in, filling the room to suffocation." In the end, a jury dismissed the murder charges and the accused went free. But for many years black Philadelphians bitterly recalled how African Americans seeking liberty were tried "under the sound of the old State House bell, and within sight of the hall where independence was declared."[16] And so the bell, facing freedom in one direction and slavery in the other, passed on to posterity.

While federal court decisions determined the fate of fugitive slaves, the work of moving the Liberty Bell from the tower proceeded. Wrestling it out of the tower and down narrow stairways was not an easy task, for only pulleys and blocks were available for handling this one-ton piece of unstable metal. It took four years. Retrieving the bell from a dark and dusty place below the steeple in the tower, the city mounted it near the first-floor entrance to Independence Hall with an elegant display. Two years later, city officials redecorated the interior of the hall.

They mounted the Liberty Bell on an ornate pedestal, a gilded American eagle perched on top. Placed at the corners of the base were eight thin columns, some surmounted by a Liberty Cap.[17] There the bell remained, a splendid display of patriotic reverence, for a quarter-century; and there it was seen by thousands of visitors who before had rarely ventured into the Independence Hall tower.

A few years later, always looking to give the icon a more history-related presence, city officials replaced the sculptured eagle sitting atop the Liberty Bell with a small stuffed eagle acquired from the natural history collection of the fabled Charles Willson Peale. This worked poorly. Many agreed that the small eagle looked ridiculous perching on the large bell, which led one visitor to offer a majestic stuffed eagle three times as large. However, the glorious eagle had only one wing. City officials saw ridicule in the offing—"a disabled eagle upon a cracked bell"— which, as an English visitor wrote in 1857, "would have afforded too many opportunities to the jibers of jibes and the jokers of jokes." So the smallish eagle, "strong, compact, and without a flaw, holds his seat upon the relic, until some more ponderous and unexceptional bird shall be permitted to dethrone him."[18]

Stardom came to the Liberty Bell in 1854, just two years after it was reinstalled on the first floor of Inde-

INTERIOR VIEW OF INDEPENDENCE HALL, PHILADELPHIA.

Max Rosenthal, *Interior View of Independence Hall*, 1855. George
Washington, at the center, commands attention, but the Liberty
Bell, with eagle astride it, was a big attraction. Many of the paintings
on the wall were from the brush of Charles Willson Peale and can be
seen today in the Second Bank of the United States in Philadelphia.
Courtesy Independence National Historical Park

pendence Hall. From this point on, mythologizing the
bell's July Fourth performance became standard practice.
Confirming and embroidering George Lippard's legend
of 1848 was another enterprising newspaperman, Joel
Tyler Headley. Replacing Lippard as the Liberty Bell's
publicity agent, he incorporated the July Fourth story in
a serialized "Life of George Washington" in *Graham's
Magazine*, published in Philadelphia. Headley pumped up
the old-man-and-flaxen-haired-lad story, confirming in

the public mind that the Old Bell had rung on the Fourth of July before an exultant mass of cheering Philadelphians and therefore was appropriately named the Liberty Bell. Not to be outdone by Lippard's melodramatic account, Headley gave the bell the ability to orchestrate its voice. Up in the steeple, he wrote,

> the old bell-man leaned over the railing, straining eyes downward, till his heart misgave him and hope yielded to fear. But at length, at two o'clock, the door of the hall opened and a voice exclaimed *"It has passed."* . . . The boy sentinel turned to the belfry, clapped his hands, and shouted, *"Ring-ring!"* The desponding bell-man, electrified into life by the joyful news, seized the iron tongue and hurled it backward and forward, with a clang that startled every heart in Philadelphia like a bugle blast. "Clang-clang" it resounded on, ever higher and clearer and more joyous, blending its deep and thrilling vibrations, and proclaiming in long and loud accents over all the land the glorious motto that encircled it. Glad messengers caught the tidings as it floated out on the air and sped off in every direction, to bear it onward.[19]

Headley's emotion-clogged Liberty Bell story reached a broad audience, for *Graham's Magazine,* previously ed-

THE BELLMAN INFORMED OF THE PASSAGE OF THE DECLARATION OF INDEPENDENCE.

J. T. Headley, "The Bellman Informed of the Passage of the Declaration of Independence," *Life of George Washington* (1858)

ited by Edgar Allan Poe, had forty thousand subscribers by this time. Though not yet a household symbol, the Liberty Bell was well on its way to becoming a precious relic to which the public could relate as a key talisman of

American freedom. In the same year that Headley re-
tailed Lippard's legend, another Philadelphia guidebook,
Things as They Are in America, confirmed that the bell had
pealed joyously on July 4, 1776. The story, it seems, was
too good to challenge. Five years later, in the first published history of Independence Hall, David W. Belisle's
spin on the graybeard man and young boy employed
near-erotic phrasing:

> Although the hand that rang [the bell] on that mem-
> orable occasion is stiff in the icy embrace of death—
> the gray-headed patriot who anxiously awaited with
> trembling hope in the belfry the signing of that Dec-
> laration, whose ejaculations—*"they'll never do it!*
> *They'll never do it!"* whose eyes dilated, whose form
> expanded, and whose grasp grew firm when the voice
> of the blue-eyed youth reached his ears in shout of
> triumph—"Ring! RING! They have signed and our
> country is free!" has been long since gathered to his
> fathers—the events of that day will commemorate
> his honor to all coming time.[20]

Belisle's 1859 account of the Liberty Bell was intended
to bring acclaim to the one-ton, cracked object, and he
certainly figured in the bell's closing in on iconic status.
Belisle was a fervent promoter of the American Party,
which railed against the incoming tide of immigrants,

and was the publisher of a party newspaper across the river in Camden. Trying to reawaken the heyday of revolutionary war patriotism, he called "the OLD STATE HOUSE BELL" the "greatest of orators the world ever knew or heard." In fact, that was just what he hoped the world would believe. "Its tongue is now still, and its voice is silent; its sides look dark and heavy, and a perceptible corrosion is indicated by chemical action of the atmosphere on its surface," he allowed. "But the peals it thundered over the land on the Fourth of July, 1776, ring with as much potency—excite as deep patriotism—awaken as strong emotions—fill the soul with as fervent love of country— inspire as holy sentiments—and thrill with as warm a glow the children of those noble patriots whose deeds gave direction to its voice, as when it proclaimed 'Liberty through the land and to all the inhabitants thereof.'"

This geyser of heart-tugging words almost assured that the Liberty Bell would now enter the nation's classrooms. Only a year after Headley's popularization of the July Fourth story, the former New England Congregational minister Charles A. Goodrich published his *Child's History of the United States*, in which he told the Liberty Bell story in words designed to enchant the young. Goodrich was a reigning author of textbooks for children—everything from *Greek Grammar* to *Bible History of Prayer* to *Lives of the Founders* to *Great Events of American History*—and his voice was authoritative. Probably half the schoolchildren in the nation had his book on their classroom desks.

Then a year after the Civil War erupted, the era's most popular songwriter, Henry Clay Work, set the Liberty Bell myth about ringing in the Declaration of Independence on July Fourth to music. Son of an abolitionist and an abolitionist himself—his Connecticut home was a stop on the Underground Railroad—Work wrote music and lyrics that thrilled the nation. Later, he would become rich by selling eight hundred thousand copies in music sheet form of "My Grandfather's Clock" (1876). But his "Ring the Bell, Watchman" had greater impact because it infused youngsters from coast to coast with bedrock patriotism. He started his song:

High in the belfry the old sexton stands,
Grasping the rope with his thin bony hands
Fix'd is his gaze as by some magic spell
Till he hears the distant murmur,
Ring, ring the bell.

Then came the chorus that more than a half-century later, according to the *Philadelphia Inquirer*, was known by "every schoolboy":

Ring the bell, watchman! Ring! Ring! Ring!
Yes, yes! The good news is now on the wing.

Yes, yes! They come and with tidings to tell
Glorious and blessing tidings. Ring, ring the bell![21]

Little could Work know that this chorus would soon produce an outpouring of patriotic sentiment because American children would soon have a chance to see the Liberty Bell up close and personal.

The election of Abraham Lincoln—and his assassination four years later—gave the Liberty Bell a new grip on the public mind. On his way from Springfield, Illinois, to take the oath of office in Washington, Lincoln had stopped in Philadelphia, where on February 22, 1861, he raised the flag at Independence Hall. Near the Liberty Bell, he spoke to a mass of Philadelphians of "the deep emotion at finding myself standing here, in this place, where were collected together the wisdom, the patriotism, the devotion to principle, from which sprang the institutions under which we live." In prophetic words he averred that "sooner than surrender these principles, I would be assassinated on this spot." Four years and two months later, he was back in Independence Hall, this time in a flag-draped casket.

Before dawn on the morning of April 22, 1865, lines began to form. By 10 A.M. the queue was three miles long. While they waited to view the body lying in state, more than a hundred thousand Philadelphians followed the funeral cortège to Independence Hall. Since the viewing hours were limited, thousands were disappointed not to see the fallen president with the mute Liberty Bell standing by. But the Liberty Bell was now all the more ennobled for its inscription, which the Great Emancipator had done so much to implement.[22]

After Lincoln's death the cause of racial justice continued to be tethered to the Liberty Bell. After all, once the bell acquired the power to move people deeply, to command their respect, awe, and even love, it was natural that those who did not yet enjoy full political or civil liberty would try to make the bell ring for them as well. Thus in 1866 Frederick Douglass, by this time the most famous African American in the United States, returned to Philadelphia to speak at the National Union Convention, which met before the midyear elections of 1866 to bridge the growing chasm between the Reconstruction policies of the Radical Republicans and President Andrew Johnson. After northerners and southerners paraded arm in arm to demonstrate national reconciliation at the Southern Loyalists Convention in 1866, Douglass invoked the Liberty Bell mystique: "I ask you . . . to adopt the principles proclaimed by yourselves, by your revolutionary fathers, and by the old bell in Independence Hall."[23]

Reaching young minds is important, almost necessary, to achieve the summit of symbolism. This certainly was the case of the Liberty Bell as the nation entered the

Gilded Age. By the 1870s the July Fourth pealing of the bell had become a staple of elementary school patriotic inculcation. George S. Hillard's widely used *Franklin's Fifth Reader* included an anonymous poem that gave the July Fourth bell-ringing story a new twist. In this rendering, the grizzled old man and young blue-eyed boy became grandfather and grandson. Recycling the old Lippard, the poem read:

> So they surged against the State House
>> While all solemnly inside
> The Continental Congress
>> Truth and reason for their guide
> O'er a simple scroll debating
>> Which, though simple it might be
> Yet should shake the cliffs of England
>> With the thunders of the free
> Far aloft in the high steeple
>> Sat the bellman, old and gray,
> He was weary of the tyrant
>> And his iron-sceptered sway.
> So he sat with one hand ready
>> On the clapper of the bell
> When his eye should catch the signal
>> The long-expected news to tell
> See! See! The dense crowd quivers

Through all its lengthy line
As the boy beside the portal
  Hastens forth to give the sign;
With his little hand uplifted,
  Breezes dallying with his hair,—
Hark! With high, clear intonation
  Breaks his young voice in the air.
Hushed the people's swelling murmur
  Whilst the boy cries joyously—
"Ring!" He shouts. "Ring, Grandpa,
  "Ring, oh ring for Liberty!"
Quickly at the given signal,
  The old bellman lifts his hand
Forth he sends the good news, making
  Iron music through the land
How they shouted! What rejoicing!
  How the old Bell shook the air
Till the clang of Freedom ruffled
  The calmly gliding Delaware!
How the bonfires and the torches
  Lighted up the night's repose
And from the flames like fabled phoenix,
  Our glorious Liberty arose!
That old State House Bell is silent
  Hushed is now its clamorous tongue,
But the spirit it awakened

Still is living—ever young;
And when we greet the smiling sunlight
On the Fourth of each July
We will ne'er forget the bellman
Who betwixt the earth and sky,
Rang out loudly "Independence!"
Which, please God, shall never die![24]

Marketing the bell was now only a matter of time, and this occurred as the nation began to heal its wounds. Just after the Civil War an enterprising Philadelphian included the Liberty Bell on an earthenware plate portraying various patriotic objects.[25] This was just the beginning. By 1876, when Philadelphia hosted the nation's hundredth birthday in a massive international Centennial Exposition, the Liberty Bell hit its stride. Perhaps only the face of George Washington could rival the Liberty Bell as a design motif, and in both cases freedom—America's gift to the world—was the point to be made. The Liberty Bell was also seen as a uniting symbol that would bind the nation's wounds and complete the process of reconciliation between North and South after the ghastly bloodletting of the previous decade. John Shoemaker, the chairman of the Centennial Committee, punched the point home:

There appears to have been no first jubilee to all the inhabitants on our fiftieth anniversary—too many

millions of our inhabitants were then in slavery—
we then could not fully carry out the text and proclaim liberty to all. But now upon the second fiftieth year, we are able to do so. Cracked and shat-
tered as the bell may be, the base upon which that
motto is cast remains firm and solid, and shaken as
has our country been with the din of battle and
bloody strife, that principle remains pure and perfect for all time to come, and the whole text, Liberty Jubilee, will be literally carried out in 1876.
"Liberty can now be proclaimed throu all the land
to all inhabitants thereof."[26]

But if the old Pass and Stow bell was "cracked and shat-
tered," what could be done to focus the attention of the
millions expected to visit the Centennial Exposition on
the nation's revered relic? Some thought the Liberty Bell
should be repaired in time to ring out at the Exposition,
but city fathers rejected this idea, doubting that any repair would restore the bell's voice and even arguing that
the sizable crack was part of its character. Some argued
the bell should have its own special building, but this too
was nixed.[27] Still, Philadelphia's patriotic citizens urged
that the bell be rung on the centennial anniversary of July
Fourth, even if its tonal quality was harsh.

It was not to be. Instead, at the fairgrounds in Fairmount Park, they saw—and heard—a gigantic reproduction of the Liberty Bell. It was the gift of a superbly talented and eccentric Philadelphian. Henry Seybert, son of a decorated Philadelphia mineralogist, chemist, congressman, and historian, became a distinguished mineralogist himself; but his absorption with spiritualism, which he believed allowed him to communicate with his deceased parents, was the real inspiration for the bell he wanted to ring out forever in the steeple of Independence Hall. His dead mother, Seybert revealed, had "begged him to buy a fine clock and bell as a gift in her memory for the old Independence Hall."[28] From this séance came Seybert's gift of $20,000 to commission a gigantic thirteen thousand–pound bell—half a ton for each original state—and a new six thousand–pound clock, with its four dials of ten feet in diameter facing the four cardinal points of the compass, to be installed in the tower of Independence Hall. The Meneely-Kimberly Foundry in upstate New York cast the bell, probably the largest ever fabricated in the United States at the time. Using four parts copper to one part tin, they added—for historic effect and to enhance the bell's power to reconcile deadly enemies—the melted-down remains of four cannon: one British and one American used in the American Revolution at the Battle of Saratoga; one Confederate and one Union from the Battle of Gettysburg. From excess bell metal the foundry fabricated hundreds of miniature souvenir bells, which the city gave to schools, thus fixing the Liberty Bell in the minds of young Americans.

Bell and clock, the latter the work of the famous Seth Thomas, were installed in time to ring out thirteen strokes on July 4, 1876, followed by thirty-eight peals for the number of American states in that year. Not satisfied with the tonal quality of the bell, Seybert ordered it recast. Called the Centennial Liberty Bell, it returned to Philadelphia in March 1877 to be rehung in the Independence Hall steeple. Ever since, it is the bell that Philadelphians and all the city's visitors hear as it strikes the hour every day of the week.[29]

Philadelphians turned out in masses to attend the Exposition, and travelers from around the nation and abroad flocked to see the spectacular array of exhibits. The Centennial Exposition married the old practice of rollicking local fairs with the new idea of international expositions: the host nation advertised its cultural and industrial accomplishments, while other nations—fifty came to the party—put on their best faces in pavilions erected in the spacious Fairmount Park. An unheard of ten million people visited the Exposition.

The opening-day crowd, claimed by one newspaper to be the "largest ever assembled on the North American continent," numbered about 186,000. One reporter said that the hotels and rooming houses that had sprung up near the fairgrounds were "as full as rabbit warrens [with] politicians of every hue and cry, and clergymen of every light and shade, doctors of great and little pills, merchants, lawyers, thieves, farmers, bankers, gamblers, showmen, shopkeepers, and every known class of man in the country." The wide-eyed Japanese commissioner to the Expo marveled at the American way of celebrating: "The first day crowds come like sheep, run here, run there, run everywhere. One man start, one thousand follow. Nobody can see anything, nobody can do anything. All rush, push, tear, shout, make plenty noise, say damn great many times, get very tired, and go home."[30]

And buy. The Liberty Bell was stamped, cast, engraved, embroidered, painted, embossed, and carved on lamps, buttons, pull toys, pillboxes, lamps, tea bells, rubber ink stamps, paperweights, dishes, goblets, medals, and toy banks. It sold as postcards, photographs, and paintings. One business-minded woman fabricated a seventy-six-piece table service, with filing fragments from an earlier attempt to repair the bell incorporated into some of the serving pieces. In the state exhibits, the Liberty Bell was reincarnated in various forms—a stone Liberty Bell from Michigan, an inlaid wood bell from Iowa, a sugar bell from Pennsylvania, and a tobacco bell from North Carolina. Only the dullest mind could miss the point: the Liberty Bell stood for patriotism, freedom, and the American way.[31]

Veneration for the Founding Fathers appeared everywhere through the Expo grounds. Nobody could walk far without seeing a statue of Washington, including one in Memorial Hall—*The Apotheosis of Washington* by an Italian sculptor in which a legless version of the *pater patriae* rode astride a gigantic eagle about to waft him aloft with the Constitution in hand. Washington even rose from the dead in a working model of his tomb, nine feet tall; toy soldiers saluted the nation's first president at regular intervals as he arose from the sepulcher. Fairgoers saw the great man more intimately through displays of Washington's military field gear and household items. The public loved the sense of intimacy they felt with the great hero when gazing at his waistcoat thrown over a chair, the folding cot spread with his blanket, the portable camp table laid for tea with salt and butter boxes and tin plates, and his rumpled regimental uniform worn when he resigned his commission to return to farming at Mount Vernon. One visitor exclaimed: "Oh what feelings I did feel as I see that coat and vest that George had buttoned up so many times over true patriotism, truthfulness, and honor. When I see the bed he had slept on, the little round table he had eat on . . . the belluses he had blowed the fire with in cold storms and discouragements. . . . Why they all

rousted up my mind so that I told Josiah I must see Independence Hall before I slept, or I wouldn't answer for the
consequences."[32]

Fired with patriotism, off to Independence Hall went
such visitors, not in a trickle but in a stream. If they hadn't
learned the lesson at the fairgrounds that the Liberty Bell
was now America's most treasured relic, they would get a
refresher course in the old city. Frank Marx Etting made
it his business to pound this home. Son of a German Jewish immigrant, Etting had served in the Civil War and
then as U.S. Army paymaster and disburser of Reconstruction funds. Even before the Civil War he had become fascinated with historical materials; in 1855, at age
twenty-two, he had become precociously a Historical Society of Pennsylvania councillor. From this springboard,
he became chief of the Centennial Exposition history
department. While fully aware of the Centennial organizers' primary goal of celebrating a century of industrial
and technological progress that was catapulting the United
States forward as a modern industrial nation, he was sure
that the Exposition provided a golden opportunity to fuse
the past with the present and the future by refreshing
public memory about the golden revolutionary age.

Etting turned the restoration of the Hall and the staging of historical exhibits there into a master plan for reha-
bilitating historical memory with a fervor matching his

pro-northern Civil War passion. "The American people," he exclaimed, "shall come to Philadelphia in 1876 to see how faithfully we have kept the sacred charge entrusted to us by our grandfathers." This required doctoring the American people who suffered from the collective disease of historical amnesia. The revolutionary era, as Etting saw it, was lost "in the mists of the past."

Anticipating that Americans from across the country and visitors from abroad would flock to Philadelphia, he centered his remedy for curing the masses of memory loss on restoring the Assembly Room to its 1776 state and then featuring the Liberty Bell (with a life-sized statue of Washington nearby) in the vestibule, where it would be the first object seen by visitors entering Independence Hall. Preparing for the crowds, carpenters suspended the bell from its original beam and scaffolding and surrounded it by an iron railing to keep people at a decent distance.[33]

Etting's love of history was matched by his imperiousness, and this almost wrecked his grandiose plans for polishing Independence Hall and its Liberty Bell as the nation's crown jewels. His first task, as he saw it, was to cleanse the layers of history deposited on the hallowed Assembly Room that had turned it into a kind of city museum—"a storehouse, a lumber-room for every variety of trash." Etting started cleaning house by stripping the room of likenesses of such Civil War heroes as Lincoln, Grant, local Union army generals; of portraits of the Mohawk chief Joseph Brant and the Seneca chief Red Jacket; of what he called the "vilest daub and caricature of General Jackson (unfit for a tavern sign)"; and of Bass Otis's painting of Thomas Paine, "an obscure political agitator doing duty for Charles Lee, of Revolutionary notoriety." This cleansing sent Etting directly into a buzz saw. Democrats were outraged that Jackson's portrait disappeared, and others believed that Lincoln and Grant vanished because Etting, with family connections in the South, wanted to ruffle no feathers of southern visitors to the Centennial.

For his troubles—he had leagued himself with Philadelphia's wealthy old families while thumbing his nose at the new legion of politicians who controlled the city's municipal government—Etting was cashiered by the city councils ten days after the July Fourth celebrations. Nonetheless, his restored rooms of Independence Hall, featuring the Liberty Bell, remained for many years as he refurnished them, including portraits of George III and other English kings (which would not be taken down until 1915). Moreover, he remained in place as chairman of the Centennial's Department of History, which gave him great power to shape the historical memory of millions of visitors.[34]

Whatever his ham-handed and politically maladroit manner, Etting put on a show at Independence Hall that wowed the public. The New Year's Eve celebration that opened the Centennial Exposition brought tens of thousands through the rain to witness Independence Hall draped with a gigantic allegorical portrait of Washington with the Goddess of Liberty hovering above him. The mayor hoisted a large replica of one of Washington's battle flags just before midnight, and at the stroke of twelve, the flag unfurled as the band struck up "The Star-Spangled Banner." The Seybert Liberty Bell pealed for thirty minutes, while inside the Hall the old Pass and Stow bell stood mute but handsomely presented. Among those who came to venerate the bell were Brazil's Emperor Dom Pedro II, the hemisphere's last monarch; and Count Rochambeau, the grandson of the French admiral whose fleet stood off the British navy at Yorktown and hastened to assure the surrender of General Cornwallis and his army in October 1781.

The Fourth of July festivities were equally extravagant. A torchlight procession trailed into the Independence Hall yard to await the stroke of midnight on July 3. Then the new tower bell began to peal. During the Fourth, the Centennial Bell was kept busy while the nation's acting vice president, Thomas W. Ferry, preached unity to a still violent nation.

But all the bell ringing, flag waving, oratorical puffery, nighttime fireworks, and cheering could not keep the famous inscription—"proclaim Liberty throughout all the Land unto all the Inhabitants thereof"—from spreading like an infection to those who did not yet enjoy the vaunted liberty claimed by patriotic white Americans. The Exposition celebrated a country reunited, but it could not disguise the political and social tensions that still remained, both between North and South and within sections, states, and cities. Everyone knew that the country was snared in the throes of a severe international depression that had begun in 1873; that Philadelphia was reeling under double-digit unemployment; and that sensational murder trials were being held nearby in Pottsville, where twenty Irish coal miners were convicted of killing mine foremen and coal company operators whom the anthracite miners had targeted as their foulest exploiters. Nor could most fairgoers ignore the headlines reporting the murderous struggle on the Great Plains, where the U.S. Army was battling the Sioux in a conflict that climaxed eight days before the monster July Fourth celebration when Crazy Horse and Sitting Bull led two thousand warriors forward to rout General George Custer and his Seventh Cavalry.

While all of these events were at a remove from Philadelphia, determined women, led by Susan B. Anthony, brought the Liberty Bell's relevance directly to the exuberant fairgoers in dramatic fashion. Women suffragists had been preparing for the Exposition, knowing that the publicity attending it gave them an unparalleled opportunity. For months they had held fund-raising and protest meetings across the nation, declaring that "to women this government is not a Republic, but a hateful oligarchy of sex." Calling for a mass protest in Philadelphia, they vowed to "declare themselves free and independent, no longer bound to obey laws in whose making they have had no voice."

The dramatic, carefully staged moment occurred on July 4 in Independence Square. Susan Anthony watched and waited as acting Vice President Ferry, a grandson of Richard Henry Lee, who a century before had proposed the resolution calling for independence, concluded his reading of the Declaration of Independence. Then Anthony pressed forward through the crowd of fifty thousand and mounted the platform with the Centennial Liberty Bell hanging high above her. Rebuffed from participating on the program, Anthony thrust a copy of the Woman's Declaration of Rights—written at the Seneca Falls Convention in 1848, where women had pushed their case for political rights—and the Articles of Impeachment Against the United States into the hands of the nonplused Ferry. With the Centennial chairman shouting

"Order, order," Anthony strode off the stage. Joining her cohorts in front of Independence Hall, where they were passing out copies of the Woman's Declaration of Rights, Anthony addressed a cheering throng: "While the nation is buoyant with patriotism, and all hearts are attuned to praise, it is with sorrow we come to strike the one discordant note. . . . We cannot forget, even in this glad hour, that while all men of every race, and clime, and condition have been invested with the full rights of citizenship under our hospitable flag, all women still suffer the degradation of disenfranchisement."[35] Did the Liberty Bell proclaim liberty for the twenty-two million women throughout the land?

Once the crowds went home from the nation's gala birthday party, the Liberty Bell, its place now assured in history, had little repose. In 1877 city officials moved the bell to the West Room opposite the Declaration chamber. Placed near a front window, where it could be seen from the street any hour of the day, the bell became a familiar sight for passers-by. But with astounding disregard for the wooden framework that carried the weight of the bell, city officials tossed it behind Independence Hall. A distraught citizen writing to the *Public Ledger*, certain that at the Centennial "millions would have given a dollar for a mere chip of those supports," asked, "Can it be possible that these timbers are now to be chopped up for firewood?" Embarrassed, the city offered the bell's trestle to the Historical Society of Pennsylvania, which regretted that it did not have room for the framework.[36]

After the centennial, the city fathers moved the bell to the stair hall beneath the Independence Hall tower, where it was suspended from a chain of thirteen massive links, each representing one of the original thirteen states.[37] There, the old Pass and Stow bell hung for nine years, its voice lost but its presence enhanced. Then, in 1885, American exposition organizers decided that the bell belonged to all Americans and therefore ought to go on the road.

THREE

On the Road with the Bell

By the time the centennial birthday party ended and the celebrants had gone home, the Liberty Bell had achieved international recognition as a symbol of freedom and a worshiped heirloom of the American Revolution. Still shrouded in myth, the bell continued to be known for ringing in the announcement of the Declaration of Independence on July 4. Lippard's legend was taken as fact in the *Dictionary of United States History*, published a half-century later under the editorship of the president of the American Historical Association, John Franklin Jameson. John H. Hazelton's scholarly *The Declaration of Independence* repeated the story in 1906.

Nothing could have better expressed the bell's intrinsic—almost magical—power than the demands that began reaching Philadelphia that the nation wanted to see *its* bell. Not everyone could visit Philadelphia, after all, so why couldn't the bell come to them? The bell was the belle of the ball, and everyone wanted to get on her dance card. Sure, Philadelphia claimed sole property interest in the bell, but that claim rang hollow once the bell was showing that it could set hearts fluttering from one side of the nation to the other.

The first of its suitors were the organizers of the New Orleans World's Industrial and Cotton Exposition in 1885. Nobody could know it at the time, but it was the first of the Liberty Bell's seven road trips between that date and 1915. "People across the country," writes the historian Charlene Mires, "serenaded the bell with patriotic tunes, reached out to touch it, and staged ceremonies that they hoped their children would long remember."[1]

Three of these trips were to former Confederate states. In each case, the exposition organizers hoped to use the Liberty Bell to demonstrate their loyalty to the reunited nation. Eager to put the Civil War behind them, southerners wanted to claim an equal role in winning independence in the American Revolution. "Our ancestors fought and bled for the time enduring principles which the bell rang out on July 4, 1776," wrote the New Orleans commissioner in charge of the Cotton Exposition there, "and, although the bell is the property of the city of Philadelphia, yet are we not co-inheritors of its glories? In the name of those mutually earned glories, we ask you to let it come to New Orleans."[2]

Philadelphia had to decide. Its mayor, William B. Smith, urged accepting the New Orleans invitation, which would show the nation that Philadelphia was eager to "set aside . . . any sectional or partisan views." Lending the bell to New Orleans would help restore "the same patriotic spirit in the entire nation at this time" and show that the City of Brotherly Love was ready to aid "in the restoration of perfect harmony throughout the nation." However, lingering concerns about the bell's safety dictated that three Philadelphia policemen should accompany the bell on its railroad trip south and guard it twenty-four hours a day.[3]

Preparing the Liberty Bell for its ride on the iron rails southward called for a special ceremony. Taken from Independence Hall, its home for 132 years, the bell was scrubbed, polished, and then taken by a flag- and bunting-covered wheeled platform drawn by six "gaily-caparisoned horses" and accompanied to the railroad station by a forty-eight-man honor guard, military battalions, and cornet bands. From there workmen hoisted it onto a flatcar fitted with special wooden railings and streamers. The bell was hung from a huge wooden yoke bearing the words "1776—Proclaim Liberty." The band played "Dixie" as the train left the West Philadelphia station on January 23, 1885.[4]

For four days, the Liberty Bell train wended its way toward New Orleans. But rather than proceeding directly southward, the train first moved westward—through the state capital at Harrisburg, then on to Pittsburgh; from there to Columbus, Ohio, and Cincinnati; then back across the Ohio River to Louisville, Kentucky, and Nashville, Tennessee. By January 25 it had reached Birmingham, Alabama, and then proceeded through Mobile and Biloxi, Mississippi, to arrive at New Orleans at noon the next day.

Crowds showed up everywhere along the route to cheer the train on. Church bells rang, cannons were fired, torches and bonfires lit up the night. At each stop, people surged forward to touch, stroke, or kiss the bell. The former president of the Confederacy, Jefferson Davis, spoke in Biloxi on behalf of the bell's power to help bind the nation's wounds. "Glorious old Bell," intoned Davis, "the son of a revolutionary soldier bows in reverence before you."[5] With hundreds of newspapers covering the train's journey to New Orleans, Americans became more and more enamored of the treasured relic of the Revolution.

The exposition organizers took no chances that the Liberty Bell wouldn't be a smashing success. To whip up interest they planted a story in local newspapers that a masked gang had overpowered and drugged the bell's

Philadelphia police guards, kidnapped the bell, hauled it to a levee, and pitched it into the Mississippi River.[6] It wasn't to be the last hoax involving the Liberty Bell.

Once installed, the Liberty Bell thrilled visitors at the New Orleans World's Industrial and Cotton Exposition for more than four and a half months. The main purpose of the exposition was to promote the economic development of the "New South" and its role, as one of the world's leading cotton producers, in the nation's march of progress. But imbedded in this message was the subtext of sectional reconciliation. As the revered symbol of American freedom, the Liberty Bell would bind former enemies together. But could that be done without embracing the South's African Americans or halting the virulent exploitation of them? The rise of the Ku Klux Klan and the Supreme Court's 1883 decisions sanctioning racial discrimination provided little hope for black Americans. So that the Liberty Bell should stand for them, too, the New Orleans directors created a Colored Department, which would erect its own building. This brought praise from Philadelphia's Henry A. Turner, bishop of the African Methodist Episcopal Church. They "stretched out their hands to us and have said: 'Come join us; we will treat you right,'" he wrote. "And they have kept their word. . . . All honor to the managers of this Exposition. All honor to New Orleans."[7]

Yet African Americans who attended the New Orleans Exposition knew that the Liberty Bell did not yet toll for them. The liberty it proclaimed throughout the land was still a bittersweet promise, not a reality. Only eleven years before, a vigilante group of some thirty-five hundred, mostly Confederate veterans—they called themselves the White League—gathered ironically in New Orleans's Liberty Place to demand that Louisiana's carpetbag governor resign. When opposed by policemen and black militia troops, the White Leaguers overwhelmed their opponents and occupied the city hall, statehouse, and arsenal. Blood ran in the streets and thirty-eight deaths and forty-one other casualties resulted from this ugly battle.

The trip home from New Orleans in June 1885 ended on a high note. Accompanied by New Orleans's mayor and other city officials, the flatcar carrying the bell followed a different route, thus giving even more Americans a chance to cheer the bell as it passed by. After rolling again through Mobile and Montgomery, Alabama, the train proceeded to Atlanta, Georgia, then headed through South Carolina and North Carolina to Baltimore, Maryland. There, members of the New Orleans party sported silver dollar–sized medals stamped with the Liberty Bell and its famous "Proclaim Liberty throughout all the Land." When the train reached Philadelphia on June 17, the city celebrated as if welcoming home a long-lost son.

An artillery unit got off 109 shots to honor the 109th year of American independence as a derrick unloaded the bell onto a horse-drawn truck, which then took it along a route smothered with flags and flowers to Independence Hall. The Centennial Bell in the steeple rang incessantly while brawny workmen restored the Liberty Bell to its place in the vestibule of Independence Hall.[8]

Two years later, the Liberty Bell had more work to do. For the hundredth anniversary of the creation of the American constitution in Philadelphia in 1787—"the masterpiece of master minds," as Hampton Carson, the Centennial Commission secretary, put it—Philadelphia's leaders wanted to educate the city's highly diverse and poorly schooled population. Trying to create a modern nationalism, they urged a worshipful stance toward the glorious past and a deeper loyalty of the masses to the state. The celebration should be upbeat, but sedate and carefully controlled. The bywords were civic unity and social harmony. The touchstones of patriotism became the Liberty Bell and the American flag (which at the time was not universally present in schoolrooms and did not command the reverence it does today).[9]

The need for this patriotic dedication was great, for the nation was in the throes of tremendous turmoil. Just the year before, in 1886, as the Constitution Centennial was being planned, a "great upheaval," as labor historians call it, rocked the United States. The flash point was a general strike in Chicago. This led to a confrontation between police and workers in Haymarket Square that left the streets running with blood. As the Centennial opened, newspapers carried screaming headlines about the conviction of the Haymarket anarchists, now scheduled for execution, while bulletins circulated about twenty thousand striking anthracite miners a day's journey from Philadelphia.

A local population of more than a million, along with some five hundred thousand visitors who slept on park benches and grassy slopes when rooms ran out, flocked to see the two processions advertised to end all processions. The first, a civic and industrial procession—replete with 21,000 paraders, 2,106 musicians, 2,099 horses, and 497 mammoth floats—was fourteen miles long. A day later a military parade with 23,732 marchers, the largest in the nation's history, featured veterans from the Grand Old Army. Thousands then flocked to see the Liberty Bell in Independence Hall, where the parade ended.[10]

The Liberty Bell now rested in Independence Hall for six years until it was summoned again for duty. The World's Columbian Exposition in Chicago (which began a year late to celebrate the four hundredth anniversary of Columbus's first voyage to the Americas) was spectacular. It lasted for six months and drew more than twenty-seven million visitors. It could hardly proceed without the Liberty Bell. The early 1890s bristled with new hereditary societies, while schoolchildren began pledging allegiance to the flag (written in 1892 by Francis Bellamy, a Christian Socialist) and immigrants immersed themselves in Americanization programs. With each state constructing a building of its own to display its citizens' talents and productivity, Pennsylvania's officials decided that the Liberty Bell should be displayed on a circular platform in the center of the state's building, surrounded by a gilt railing to keep at a respectable distance those eager to caress it. With the bell now truly a national icon, the Pennsylvanians took care to ensure against the possibility of fire: the platform was placed on specially fabricated rollers that would allow for an emergency exit from the building.[11]

Eager to have the bell receive the applause of millions of Americans along the route west, Philadelphia officials allowed a week of travel before the Chicago extravaganza opened on May 1, 1893. Even leaving Philadelphia became an occasion for worship. As if the Liberty Bell would never return, thousands of Philadelphians thronged Independence Hall as workers prepared to remove the bell. "Fathers with their little sons, mothers with babes in their arms, the gaily dressed promenaders, shop girls, clerks, and business men alike," reported the *Public Ledger*, "were eager to file past the sacred relic." Then followed the pa-

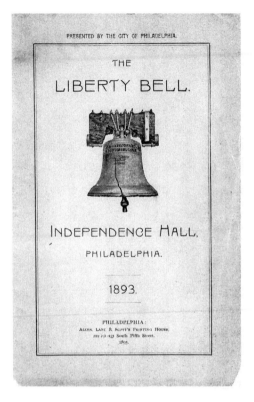

Souvenir pamphlet for Chicago World's Fair, 1893. The South was still
not willing to accept the American flag as something to revere, in spite of
the "flags in classrooms" campaign under way; but they saw the Liberty
Bell differently, as a symbol of the nation's birth that they could venerate.
Courtesy Independence National Historical Park

rade to the station. Drawn by six horses and escorted by a
city police troop, the bell reached the station in time to
leave at 10 A.M.[12]

Along the way west, the bell was "one continuous
inspiration to patriotism," as a Philadelphia newspaper

crowed.[13] Stopping in towns large and small, the train carrying the bell was pelted with floral tributes and greeted by flocks of schoolchildren, whose textbooks had been busily promoting the Lippard legend. At Oil City thirteen tots presented thirteen baskets of roses to garland the bell. At towns where the train could not afford the time to stop during the night, people lit huge bonfires so that the throngs could see the Liberty Bell as it majestically rumbled through their towns. In Indianapolis, the city's *Journal* caught the cascading importance of the bell as a symbol of civic religion:

> In reality, it is nothing but a rough and cracked old bell, nothing like as large or handsome as hundreds of others throughout the country. Yet to every intelligent and patriotic American it is worth infinitely more than all the rest. They would fight for it. If necessary they would go to war to protect it or to rescue it from an invader. . . . Why? Because it represents a sentiment and an idea that Americans would die for. The American imagination has invested it with a dignity that makes it sacred and with something like a personality that endears it to every man, woman and child who knows its history.[14]

After thrilling immense crowds in Pittsburgh, Cleveland, Columbus, and Indianapolis—"amid the thunderous acclaim of multitudes whose enthusiasm the rain could not damp," reported the *New York Times*—the Liberty Bell pulled into Chicago on Friday, April 28, at 9 P.M. The next morning, thirteen black horses with one hundred equestrian Chicago Hussars, an elite unit of the Illinois National Guard, escorted the bell to the "White City," where hundreds of buildings had been erected on the marshlands of Lake Michigan seven miles south of the Loop.[15]

This was to be not a military parade but a popular parade because, as the Columbian Exposition Committee on Arrangements argued, "as the Independence Bell was and is the people's bell, so the procession should be a procession of the people in its honor." One Chicago newspaper, reporting on the procession that stretched for two miles, called it "one grand march through crowds of enthusiastic people who cheered the Emblem of Liberty every step of the way—greater homage was never paid King or Queen."[16]

But if it was the idol of an American people's procession, the Liberty Bell was also becoming the property of an international constituency as a result of its exposure in Chicago. While escalating industrial output and territorial expansion were gaining the United States recognition as a world power, the Liberty Bell and its message of freedom became one of the nation's key exports. Not everyone saw the coup of American sugar planters in Hawaii to overthrow and imprison Queen Liliuokalani—a regime change implemented by American gunboats just months before the Chicago Exposition opened—as the extension of freedom. But nonetheless, Americans—and overseas visitors as well—began to see the Liberty Bell as an avatar for worldwide freedom from tyranny and oppression.

It is not clear that these were the thoughts of the "exotics" brought from great distances to Chicago. Nobody has quite figured out what was on the mind of the "Esquimaux" who visited from far north or "natives from Tehuantepec" from far south of the border or "dusky-skinned men and women from Samoa." Such visitations were arranged to show the world that the country welcomed people from every corner of the earth to witness the marvels of American civilization.[17] Also, the presence of dark-skinned distant people fed into the missionary crusade that was sweeping the country as a way of bearing the "white man's burden."

For six months, the Liberty Bell held court. On opening day, at least twenty-five thousand came to the Pennsylvania Building to see the bell—more than to any other state building. Throughout its visit, it was closely guarded by a battalion of Philadelphia policemen. Then on July 4, 1893, came the climax. A band hammered out the "Liberty Bell March," the latest martial composition from

America's bandmaster, John Philip Sousa. Softer tones came from Madge Morris Wagner, a California romantic poetess who composed "Liberty's Bell" for the occasion:

Men laughed in derision, and scoffed at the pains
Of the builders; and harder and harder the chimes
Of a tyrannous might on the people were laid.
More insatiate, more servile, the tribute they paid,
There was something found far more cruel than
    death,
And something far sweeter than life's fleeting
    breath.

But hark! In the midst of a turbulent throng,
The moans of the weak, and the groans of the
    strong,
There's a cry of alarm. Some invisible power
Is moving the long-silent bell in the tower
Forward and backward! And forward it swung,
And Liberty! Liberty! Liberty! Rung
From its wide brazen throat, over mountain and vale,
Till the seas caught the echo, and monarchs turned
    pale.

Our forefathers heard it—that wild, thrilling tone,
Crying out to the world, and they claimed it their
    own.

And up from the valley, and down from the hill
From the flame of the forge, from the field, and the
  mill,
They paid with their lives, the price of its due,
And left it a legacy, freeman, to you.

If Wagner's poetry hardly makes today's readers trem-
ble, it was enough at the time to inspire the Daughters of
the American Revolution to commission a gigantic replica
of the Liberty Bell. Built of melted down objects with
historical character and cast at an eye-blinking weight of
thirteen thousand pounds—one thousand for each of the
original thirteen states—the Columbian Liberty Bell attracted much attention at the Exposition. Included among
the smelted silver, gold, nickel, bronze, and copper objects from which it was cast were copper pennies said to
be current when Christ was on earth, pike heads used by
John Brown's Christian soldiers at Harper's Ferry, a silver
spoon used by John C. Calhoun, hinges from a door in
Abraham Lincoln's Springfield, Illinois, house, links of
George Washington's surveying chain, a copper kettle
once belonging to Thomas Jefferson, the abolitionist
and suffragist Lucretia Mott's silver fruit knife, and a
multitude of silver thimbles. Hoping to use the bell as a
"missionary of freedom," the DAR added to the familiar
"Proclaim Liberty" inscription two others from the Bible:

"Glory to God in the Highest, and on earth peace, good will toward men" (Luke 2:14) and "A new commandment I give unto you, that ye love one another" (John 13:34).[18]

After the Exposition closed, the DAR's Columbian Liberty Bell traveled the country for seven years. Then it made its way to Europe for the Paris World's Exhibition in 1900, which introduced the world to Art Nouveau architecture and design. Sometime after that it disappeared. According to one source, it was seized by the tsarist government in Russia about 1905 and was later melted down by Bolsheviks for weapons and ammunition in the 1917 revolution.[19]

On July Fourth, 1893, the Liberty Bell reached the pitch of its six-month visit to Chicago. The head of the 1887 Philadelphia Constitution Centennial, Hampton L. Carson, spared no hyperbole in the White City. After an enormous parade that stretched for miles, he stood at the podium and modestly called it the most momentous day "in ten thousand years of recorded history." The modern Plutarch, he vowed, would record the morning's procession as epochal. "No Paulus Aemilius, crowned with Delphic laurel, nor ambitious Pompey, decked with the spoils of plundered provinces, appeared in that procession. No wailing victims of the fate of war were there to grace in captive bonds the conqueror's chariot wheels; no bullocks were led out to slaughter; no savage games were thrown open to the people, where tigers, famished into madness, tore the flesh of men but little less ferocious than themselves." No, none of that. Instead, in the shadow of the Liberty Bell, "the *Io Triumphe* of the American people rang out above the heads of the marching squadrons as they wound their glittering length through your great highways, to bow in reverence at the shrine of the Constitution of liberty, of order, and of law. Not on the Field of the Cloth of Gold, the Champ de Mars, nor even in Trafalgar Square; not in Venice, in her days of glory, nor yet in the Crescent City by the Golden Horn, was ever witnessed such a convocation of mankind." And they were all there—"all classes and conditions of persons, of all sects and creeds, of all nationalities, of all ranks and stations"—to "testify their allegiance to the Constitution and to the flag of the United States, and . . . to assert the truth of their belief that in that Constitution there was granted to man the noblest and the freest chart of government that either ancient or modern times can boast." Then, playing schoolteacher, Carson related the history of the Liberty Bell and, along the way, set the facts straight: the old Pass and Stow bell never tolled on July Fourth but did so on July Eighth; and nowhere in his account was the old man, or grandfather, moved into a burst of bell ringing by the young boy, or grandson. Now iconic, the hoary legend of George Lippard could be safely put to rest. Nonetheless, the Liberty Bell retained its capacity to tug at the hearts of the masses.

Carson ended with rhetorical allusions to two millennia of world history that he hoped would convince all who listened of the international importance of the Liberty Bell. Since it could not travel abroad, he proclaimed, the bell's message of universal liberty must be carried by the gigantic Columbian Liberty Bell, scheduled to be the overseas missionary.

> Thou, great Bell! Cast from the chains of liberators and the copper pennies of the children of our public schools, from sacred relics contributed by pious and patriotic hands, . . . And consecrated by the prayers of the American people, take up the note of prophecy and of jubilee rung out by your older sister in 1776, and in your journey round the globe proclaim from mountain top and valley, across winding river and expansive sea, those tones which shall make thrones topple and despots tremble in their sleep, until all peoples and all nationalities, from turbaned Turks and Slavic peasants to distant islanders and the children of the Sun, shall join in the swelling chorus, and the darkest regions of the earth shall be illumed by the heaven-born light of Civil and Religious Liberty![20]

After the July Fourth extravaganza, shoals of visitors poured into the Pennsylvania building to see the Liberty Bell. Did African Americans come as much as whites? The bell's inscription had been much bandied about as the catchphrase of an advanced democracy; but what did it mean to those not yet favored with the political liberty and social justice enjoyed by white citizens? In the main, black visitors paid their respects to the Liberty Bell, partly because the Chicago World's Fair did more to be inclusive than had the Philadelphia expositions of 1876 and 1887 and far more than the New Orleans Exposition of 1885. One of the main attempts to honor blacks was the Haytian Pavilion, where Frederick Douglass held court almost daily for six months. Perhaps even more important was the eight-day Congress on Africa, where black theologians, intellectuals, and political leaders debated the future of the sons and daughters of the diaspora and devised strategies to force reluctant white Americans to grant the full rights that the Liberty Bell proclaimed as universal. Some regarded the Colored American Day, on August 25, 1893, as racist and tokenistic, but others saw it as a chance to display race achievement.[21]

For a farewell stage call, the Pennsylvania commissioners planned for the Liberty Bell to ring, if only discordantly, at the closing ceremonies on October 28. But these plans were canceled when a disappointed office seeker lurking in the crowd assassinated Chicago's mayor, Carter H. Harrison, just after the Mayor of the Common Man, as he was known, finished his Exposition-closing address. So amid sadness, the bell, aglow with praise from the millions who saw it, began its sojourn back to Philadelphia through Indiana, Ohio, and the breadth of Pennsylvania. Philadelphia's *Public Ledger* crowed about the bell's "triumphal progress" homeward. All along the way schoolchildren turned out to see the bell. In Cincinnati thirty thousand of them trooped by the bell on "Liberty Bell Day," singing patriotic songs including "Ring the Bell," the song created a generation before.[22] We can only imagine how, many years later, they passed along to their children and grandchildren the story of this moment in their humdrum schooldays.

The route of the bell took it through Pittsburgh and Pennsylvania's capital at Harrisburg en route to a stop in Allentown, where it had been secreted 116 years before to keep it out of British hands. But first it had to pass through Reading. As the bell train approached, townspeople and farmers from all around lined the tracks for miles to usher the train into town. Cannon discharges, fireworks, factory whistles and "people who yelled themselves hoarse" brought the train into the terminal. With ten thousand schoolchildren among a throng that outnumbered the town's population, the police struggled to maintain control, "but they might just as well have been egg shells under a pile driver." Pulling into Allentown for a nighttime celebration, the bell received the usual flower pelting from enthusiasts. It would have taken near-death to keep any Allentown resident away from the parade and fireworks that accompanied the occasion.[23]

By the time the bell reached Philadelphia on November 6, 1893, some twenty million Americans—about one-third of the nation—had gazed at it. Flag worship had seized the country in an era of mass immigration, and bell worship now became its cousin. After a hundred thousand Philadelphians thronged the procession from the train station to Independence Hall, Mayor Edwin S. Stuart welcomed the bell home, boasting, "There is not money enough in the world to buy from us our sacred relic of the country's liberty, and with the citizens of the nation at our backs, there is no army in the world that could wrest it from us." Not even a ferocious nor'easter storm could stop an emotional crowd from surging forward to touch and kiss the bell as workmen wrestled it into Independence Hall. When the public was done with its welcome-home effusions, they put the bell into position, attached it to the thirteen-link chain that hung from the ceiling, and hoisted it to its former place.[24]

Philadelphia's officials by now knew that they possessed something akin to the Rosetta Stone. This relic required special treatment, especially after the bell's private watchman was found chipping off small pieces and selling them as souvenirs. City officials had the bell installed in a highly decorated protected oak case in the vestibule of Independence Hall. Over the case stood a wooden eagle called "Old Abe," after the Wisconsin war eagle that had followed a Union regiment through thirty-six battles in the Civil War.[25]

The Liberty Bell had hardly assumed its new location in Independence Hall in 1894 before its peregrinations began again. Despite fears that life for it might end in a railroad smash-up, city officials wanted the bell to travel. They found support from a court ruling that agreed that while the bell was the city's property, no good argument had been brought forward to deny its traveling rights. "The bell is not a thing to be laid up in lavender, impounded, and like a grand Lama, secreted forever in the dim seclusion of Independence Hall," opined an editorialist in the *Philadelphia Inquirer.*[26]

During a difficult decade of severe depression and racial discord, the court ruling virtually made if not the bell itself, then at least its power to spark patriotism, the property of the entire nation. And so the bell went to Atlanta for the Cotton States and International Exposition in 1895. Everywhere along the route southward, people flocked to see it. "Like a benediction," reported Philadelphia's *Public Record*, the Liberty Bell rolled through the Roanoke Valley, over the rugged Blue Ridge Mountains, and down through the valley of east Tennessee "on this ideal Sabbath." At a whistle-stop in tiny Elliston, Virginia, a seventy-year-old great-grandson of Patrick Henry "pressed forward and craved permission to touch the Bell." In Bristol, Tennessee, an eighty-eight-year-old woman fell on her knees before the bell and "invoked a Divine blessing upon the old mass of historic iron."[27]

When the train reached the Atlanta depot on October 8, 1895, the aura the bell created astounded even the exposition directors, who had planned a public holiday for its arrival. For two miles, the bell train slowly chugged through walls of cheering Georgians as every steam whistle in the city shrieked its welcome. The crowd broke through guardrails and rushed to the flatcar to touch the bell. "Several children, held up by their parents," reported the *Atlanta Constitution*, "kissed the revered old bell and happily patted its great brazen sides, hardly knowing what they were doing or why, but feeling, as all present did, that electric thrill of self-satisfaction and national pride." The city's schoolchildren, having been told about the bell's history, were given city transit discounts to get to the fair. For good luck, boys rubbed coins over its surface, and a blind child was held up to pass his fingers over the inscription.[28]

Amid the featured industrial and agricultural exhibits that dotted the Exposition in Piedmont Park, the speech of Booker T. Washington was notable—and, as it turned out, historic. Invited to give one of the opening addresses in the hope it would produce an impression of racial harmony— the South was in the midst of a wave of lynchings—Washington proposed what was to be called the Atlanta Compromise. The founder and principal of Tuskegee Institute in Alabama urged his fellow African Americans to reach accommodation with white power, content to follow farming and vocational skilled trades rather than challenge the social and political supremacy of white southerners. "Cast down your buckets where you are," counseled Washington, "by making friends in every manly way of the people of all races by whom we are surrounded." If anyone noticed the contradiction between the Liberty Bell's famous inscription and Washington's public statements that black Americans should not at that time pursue the vote or civil rights, no one said so at the time. Criticism would come later, led by the young W. E. B. Du Bois, but for now most whites and blacks welcomed Washington's attempt to bring racial reconciliation to the country while not challenging racial inequality.

On the way home, the Liberty Bell snaked its way up the Atlantic seaboard in January 1896, saluted, garlanded, kissed, and prayed over at dozens of whistle-stops. On

February 1 it reached Philadelphia, where its restoration to Independence Hall was saluted by the speeches and parades that were now almost obligatory whenever the bell came home. Back to the glass case in the Assembly Room it went. By now civic leaders understood that expositions had become a source of great profit, and nobody wanted an exposition without the revered Liberty Bell. But Philadelphia's leaders, worried that the wear and tear of jaunts across the country might imperil the bell, put their foot down. It was "no" to Nashville, Tennessee, for its 1897 Tennessee Centennial Exposition; "no" to Omaha, Nebraska, for the Trans-Mississippi and International Exposition in 1898; "no" to Boston for the 125th anniversary in 1900 of the Battle of Bunker Hill; "no" to the Paris International Exposition in the same year; and "no" to the Buffalo, New York, Pan-American Exposition in 1901.

But as the nation's most eminent goodwill ambassador, the Liberty Bell could not be refused to everyone. A request from Charleston, South Carolina, for the bell to take up residence at the Carolina Inter-State and West Indian Exposition in 1902—again the argument was for patriotism and sectional unity—finally drew the Liberty Bell out of Independence Hall again. On the trip southward, the bell received the usual accolades, and schoolchildren, by this time rehearsed in the Liberty Bell's history in every corner of the nation at a time of expansionist

American chauvinism, sang patriotic songs, threw flowers at the bell, and wrote essays about it.

After almost six months in Charleston, where hundreds of thousands gazed at the bell in the Pennsylvania Building, the bell returned home in June 1902. At a stop in Washington, D.C., the marine band played Sousa's "Liberty Bell March." After the bell reached Philadelphia on June 10, 1902, one city father summed up its extraordinary power at the dawn of the twentieth century:

> This Bell should be, and has been, an inspiration
> of patriotism in all the towns through which we
> have passed on our journey from the Charleston
> fair. Thousands of people have flocked to see it
> throughout the South, not in Charleston alone, but
> at every point where we have stopped for even the
> smallest length of time. That the significance of this
> relic is appreciated through the South and the love
> of liberty throughout the South is as strong today as
> it was in the stirring times when this piece of brazen
> metal proclaimed freedom to the world.[29]

After only one year resting at home, the Liberty Bell made its first and only trip northward to the cradle of American independence, Boston. It was also its shortest stay-over at another city, only five days. Three years after Boston officials had unsuccessfully requested the bell,

Kissing the bell, Charleston, SC, 1902. Nobody counted the number of children held up by parents and grandparents to kiss the Liberty Bell, but the number was vast. It is safe to say that few children forgot the experience, passing the story on to their own children and grandchildren. Bell kissing was important in the rise of the Liberty Bell to iconic status. Courtesy Independence National Historical Park

Philadelphia officials obliged for the 128th anniversary of Bunker Hill. Leaving Philadelphia in mid-June, aflutter with flowers, bunting, and flags, it passed through countless towns in New Jersey, New York, Connecticut, Rhode Island, and Massachusetts. At Princeton Junction, on the mainline from Philadelphia to New York, it made a side trip to Princeton for a twenty-minute stop, enough for the entire town and gown to turn out. As the train proceeded north, immense crowds turned out all along the route. In New Haven, Connecticut, home of Yale University, twenty thousand walked around the bell. "I believe the Bell is the greatest educator of Patriotism we have," wrote one New Haven official. "The gray-haired old veteran and the small school child are alike in their anxiety to touch this sacred old relic of Revolutionary days and the old herald of Liberty."[30]

Once it reached Boston, the Liberty Bell was joined by a small bell owned by John Brown—a reminder that abolitionists six decades before had given the bell its enduring name. The bell was the main attraction of the parade from South Station to Charlestown, site of the historic battle. On a float drawn by thirteen bay horses and escorted by the Ancient and Honorable Artillery Company, the bell took its place next to the Bunker Hill monument. After only two days, it was back on the flatcar for the return home. As usual, Philadelphians turned out to welcome the bell back. Since 1900 it had been relocated within Independence Hall; now it was enclosed in a glass barrier, near the grand staircase on the first floor.

The bell was hardly back in Philadelphia before it inspired another kind of freedom tour. A few weeks before the Liberty Bell train chugged out of the city, headed for Boston, Mary Harris Jones, known as Mother Jones, had assembled a pitiful cadre of preteenage boys and girls who toiled in the Kensington textile mills. Gathering them in front of Independence Hall, she "held up their mutilated hands"—mangled in the assembly line machines—as evidence that "Philadelphia's mansions were built on the broken bones, the quivering hearts, and drooping heads of these children." Then, on July Fourth, 1903, the Liberty Bell's return to the city inspired a new tactic for bringing the exploitation of child labor before the nation. "The Liberty Bell that a century ago rang out for freedom against tyranny was touring the country," Mother Jones wrote, "and crowds were coming to see it everywhere. That gave me an idea. These little children were striking for some of the freedom that childhood ought to have, and I decided that the children and I would go on a tour." Thus began Mother Jones's Children's March. For twenty days her bedraggled army of children with "puny arms and legs and hollow chests" walked northward for 125 miles to confront President Teddy Roosevelt at his Oyster Bay, Long Island, mansion. Along the way, at Princeton, New Jersey, they stayed in "the big cool barn on Grover Cleveland's great estate" and then stood by Mother Jones before Princeton University's faculty and students while she told the university crowd "that the rich robbed these little children of any education of the lowest order that they might send their sons and daughters to places of higher education. That they used the hands and feet of little children that they might buy auto-

large cities such as Milwaukee and Minneapolis the train tarried for three hours or more. On the final leg, the bell train whistle-stopped through Iowa and Illinois, to arrive in St. Louis after nearly six days on the road.

Of all the expositions that had charmed Americans since 1876, the St. Louis Exposition topped them all. More than nineteen million visitors saw automobiles aplenty in the early days of car manufacturing. They marveled at airships, savored a new treat called the ice cream cone, peered at a reproduction of Abraham Lincoln's boyhood cabin and a tavern used by Washington during the American Revolution. They cheered lustily at the first Olympic Games held in the Western Hemisphere and gawked at a twenty-foot-tall equestrian knight made of prunes from the Santa Clara Valley in northern California. But one of the most powerful messages of the Exposition came from displaying what the promoters believed were evolutionist concepts by assembling indigenous people from around the world, who lived for many weeks in their re-created native villages. If visitors hadn't absorbed Darwin's theory of natural selection and the survival of the fittest, it was all—purportedly—on view here: "a vast museum of anthropology and ethnology" including Mbuti Pygmies from the Congo; heavily tattooed Cocopas from Sonora, Mexico; gigantic Patagonian Tehuelches; and "hairy" bear-worshiping Ainus from a remote corner of East Asia. Here was a way of celebrating the assumed cultural superiority of western Europeans and their American cousins.[32]

But for all of this, the Liberty Bell not only held its own but was a gigantic attraction. It had its own day—Liberty Bell Day on June 8—replete with a six-mile parade along streets lined with schoolchildren who had been given the day off to see the bell. Resting on a blanket of American flags in the Pennsylvania Building, the bell confirmed the claim of one orator that "next to the manuscript of the immortal Declaration of Independence, this bell is the one object best known and revered by the American people."[33]

Once the bell was back in Philadelphia, citizen groups and politicians vowed to keep it home. Finding in early 1909 that the bell's crack (hairline and almost imperceptible) had lengthened by seventeen inches, city fathers were now facing a request from San Francisco to bring the bell there for the Panama-Pacific Exposition scheduled for 1915. Local newspapers would have none of it. "Independence Hall is the place for the Liberty Bell," editorialized the *Public Ledger*, and Philadelphia would see to it that "the journeying and junketing days of that priceless relic of the Revolution are ended forever." Not denying the commercial value of the bell's presence at home, the city paper allowed that "considered merely as an advertisement for Philadelphia, the place for the bell is in Philadelphia and nowhere else." But fear also was mounting that the bell, with its longer crack, would suffer some further mishap. It would be the city's eternal shame if the "national relic, almost as precious to America as is Magna Charta to Great Britain," were damaged or, to conjure the worst, destroyed. But the *New York Times* countered that the Liberty Bell had incalculable "lessons of history" to tell, especially to "young people, to think and study in a way that cannot have other than good results."[34]

The United States had not yet entered World War I, but the international storm clouds already gathering magnified the role of the Liberty Bell as an international symbol of freedom. That iconic status was one of the reasons why the organizers of the Panama-Pacific International Exposition wanted the bell. They had planned the extravaganza to commemorate the completion of the Panama Canal in 1914—called the "Thirteenth Labor of Hercules"—and also to celebrate San Francisco's rebirth after the city had suffered a devastating earthquake and fire in 1906. Since the bell had never been west of St. Louis and the population of the western states had grown spectacularly, the presence of the bell would be like a gigantic magnet attracting millions of filings into its field of force. The official historian of the Exposition made that plain:

"Few incidents in the Exposition's growth aroused deeper and wider interest than the agitation to bring the Liberty Bell across the continent."[35]

The patriotic value of having the Liberty Bell as an especially honored guest had a new twist. At the West Coast's point of entry for immigrants from Asia, and the site of virulent anti-Chinese and anti-Japanese sentiment that went back almost half a century, the bell could play an important role in "Americanizing" the Asians, imagined as an inferior and alien people. Indeed, with immigration reaching new heights in the country, the need to inculcate the alien masses, as well as all schoolchildren, with American values was heartfelt.

Playing on the bell's influence in turning children into patriotic citizens for three decades of expositions, San Francisco's directors adopted the St. Louis strategy of placing schoolchildren in the role of supplicants to the bell's keepers. But San Francisco did even better. Organizers, launching their campaign even before the outbreak of World War I, set October 11, 1912, as Liberty Bell Day. Throughout the city, schoolteachers conducted readings about the bell, then asked the children to sign a petition imploring the mayor and councilmen of Philadelphia to send the bell west. Even in the segregated Oriental School of San Francisco, the Chinese and Japanese children added their names. Up and down the state, teachers put the same petition before their students. Pasted together, the petitions, with about 250,000 signatures, stretched two miles long. Wound on a large reel, it traveled east after a festive parade in San Francisco on Thanksgiving Day to be presented in Philadelphia on December 7, 1912. Reaching mayors of scores of towns and cities through which the Liberty Bell would pass, San Francisco officials urged them to lobby Philadelphia officials, stressing that a trip across the country and back would affect the "broadening and deepening [of] the spirit of patriotism in hundreds of thousands of hearts of those loyal Americans who have honored it and revered it for its place in American history, but who otherwise would never have an opportunity of beholding it."[36]

Philadelphians, however, were tired of sending their bell on what seemed to be never-ending trips, and some were sure that for all the talk about the bell's importance in promoting patriotism, the real motive was to obtain an attraction with proven ability to bring masses of fairgoers to the exposition grounds and thus to ensure the profitability of the fair and its army of vendors. Independence Hall's curator also worried that every time the bell went on the road, it came back lighter by the weight of a few dozen gouged souvenirs. "At least 25 pounds of it from time to time has been maliciously cold-chiseled off the lip of the bell," lamented Wilfred Jordan, and "on the aver-

The scroll on the car reads: "Panama-Pacific International Exposition, School Children's Petition Liberty Bell, 1915." From the collection of Donna Ewald Huggins

age of three times a year, people call here with what they claim to be a piece of the Liberty Bell metal."[37]

Such cynicism notwithstanding, Philadelphia officials decided to arrange one more pilgrimage for their treasured bell. The decision was made painfully in 1914 amid much petitioning to keep the bell in Philadelphia and concerns about the bell's capacity to withstand another long trip. By this time World War I had exploded, though the United States, under President Woodrow Wilson's policy of neutrality, had remained on the sidelines. With war fever increasing, the urgency of patriotism was all the more evident. Thus sending the Liberty Bell to the West Coast became an ever more compelling idea.

Finally, in January 1915, Philadelphia's mayor, Rudolph Blankenburg, holding the naysayers at bay, approved the plan. Looking back at the effort to overcome the recalcitrance of Philadelphia's officials, the San Francisco Exposition historian wrote, "Few incidents in our recent history have done more than the result of that agitation [over bringing the bell west] to stimulate patriotism and bring the public mind to dwell on the traditions of independence and democracy that form the best inheritance of the Americas."[38] He was right. The trip was the grand crescendo of the Liberty Bell's seven road trips.

But before that final road trip, the bell had another historic role to play—what Philadelphia's *Public Ledger* called "a telephonic journey." The Liberty Bell was chosen to demonstrate the linking by transcontinental telephone of the American people living on the shores of the Atlantic and Pacific oceans. The first message heard in San Francisco from Philadelphia, on February 11, 1915, was the sound of three wooden mallets striking the Liberty Bell. "When I struck the Bell, with the little wooden mallet," recounted the head of Philadelphia's Bureau of City Property, "there was a second of suspense while we listened with straining ears. Gradually the vibrations swelled until they merged into a harsh rumble that could be placed nowhere in the musical scale. . . . There was no mellowness in the tone, but there was a slight ringing quality." Captured by phonographic record, the moment ushered the Liberty Bell into the heady new century of technological innovation. Though far from melodious, the long-silenced voice of the bell had been restored—across the country.[39]

Three months later, after the German navy had torpedoed the *Lusitania* on May 7, 1915, the nation edged closer to war. In a time of great uncertainty, metal experts installed a "spider" to stabilize the bell. That done, Philadelphians gave their precious relic a rousing July 4 send-off, with military regiments, mounted city troopers, and—for the first time—a motorcade accompanying the bell to the train station. One Philadelphia newspaper reported a nearly frenzied goodbye throng: "Women jumped the ropes and forced armfuls of flowers upon the big fellows [troopers]. They blushed like schoolboys, shouldered them, saluted and marched on, smiling at the thousands who, raising their hats, cheered the Bell's escort and the clanking soldiers."[40]

But even as some Philadelphia women were giving the treasured Liberty Bell a gaudy sendoff, others were mounting a campaign to commission a replica Liberty Bell to

Opening transcontinental telephone service, January 25, 1915.
Policemen stand by as the Philadelphia mayor taps the Liberty
Bell to inaugurate the telephone service linking the East and West
coasts. Courtesy Independence National Historical Park

serve the woman's suffrage crusade. From the time Susan
B. Anthony had stood before Independence Hall in 1876
to read the Women's Declaration of Rights and Articles
of Impeachment Against the United States, women had

seen that they could hitch their star to the Liberty Bell. Knowing that the Liberty Bell would soon be traveling west, through many states that had already extended the vote to women, Pennsylvania suffragists, spearheaded by Katherine Wentworth Ruschenberger, arranged to cast a Liberty Bell of their own. But they added two words to the famous inscription: the bell would not only proclaim liberty throughout the land but "establish justice," which meant enfranchising women. Thus it became known as the Justice Bell.

Women of the Pennsylvania Woman Suffrage Association, who supported most Progressive programs such as prohibition, access to birth control, urban settlement houses, and child-labor laws, led the movement. Chaining the bell's clapper to its side, to peal only after women achieved the vote, women toured the bell through all sixty-seven counties in Pennsylvania to persuade voters to "proclaim the political independence of [women] throughout the State." Draping the bell in yellow and black, the colors of the women's suffrage movement, Ruschenberger belted out her punch line from one end of the state to the other: "The original Liberty Bell announced the creation of democracy; the Woman's Liberty Bell will announce the completion of democracy."[41]

Though rural Pennsylvanians, conservative for the most part, had little use for the Justice Bell, Philadelphians applauded it. The *Philadelphia Inquirer*, Republican on most issues, celebrated the bell for its devotion to "Justice, not abstract justice, but justice for the downtrodden women of this country who are now crushed under the iron heel of male domination."[42] As the November election neared, in which Pennsylvanians would vote on a suffrage amendment to the state constitution, hundreds of newspapers carried the rhyming message: "Father, brother, husband, son. Vote for Amendment #1."

The amendment failed—narrowly—and the clapper remained mute, chained to the bell's side, but the national crusade to amend the U.S. Constitution continued in the midst of a ghastly war in the trenches of western Europe. Finally the moment came. Ratification of the Nineteenth Amendment on August 26, 1920, gave the Justice Bell its moment of triumph. For the ceremony in Philadelphia women brought their bell to Independence Hall. A month after the ratification was sealed, women gathered in force, along with male supporters, to release the clapper and set it pealing joyously. For seven months the Justice Bell remained on a platform outside Independence Hall. But in February 1921 city officials, arguing that people would be confused by two bells resting near each other, evicted it. Ruschenberger later gave the bell to the Washington Memorial Chapel at Valley Forge, where visitors can still see it in the bell tower.

The Woman's Liberty Bell

Silent Until November 2nd

1776
LIBERTY

1915
EQUALITY

"LIBERTY THROUGHOUT THE LAND TO ALL THE INHABITANTS THEREOF"
Was the Message of
THE LIBERTY BELL OF 1776

It proclaimed the birth of a new nation "DEDICATED TO THE PROPOSI-
TION THAT JUST GOVERNMENTS DERIVE THEIR POWER FROM
THE CONSENT OF THE GOVERNED" AND THAT "TAXATION WITH-
OUT REPRESENTATION IS TYRANNY."

Today, fifty million of these inhabitants are women, but only four million of
them have received the full benefits of the Liberty which the old bell proclaimed.
These four million women live in the equal suffrage states of the West and Middle
West. The people of these states think as did Abraham Lincoln who said:
"I GO FOR ALL SHARING THE PRIVILEGES OF
GOVERNMENT WHO ASSIST IN BEARING ITS
BURDENS, BY NO MEANS EXCLUDING WOMEN"

Even as the original Liberty Bell rang first for Pennsylvania in 1776 so
should the new Liberty Bell proclaim a new message of Liberty first in Pennsylvania this year. The new bell is the Woman's Liberty Bell, which is to ring
for the first time on the day that the Women of Pennsylvania are granted the
right to vote. Every fair-minded man in Pennsylvania will help to make this day
November second next

Because every fairminded man believes in Justice and
Because Justice is an empty word so long as half the population
of a Commonwealth have no say in the making of its laws.
The Liberty Bell of 1915 rang to "proclaim Liberty" to create our nation.
The Woman's Liberty Bell will ring to "establish justice"—to complete
our nation.

Help break the chains that hold the bronze clapper silent.
Vote "Yes" on the Suffrage Amendment on Election Day.

Pennsylvania Woman Suffrage Association
Campaign Headquarters:—201 Arcade Building, Harrisburg, Pennsylvania

Woman's Liberty Bell poster. For all their importance to the Progressive
Movement, women did not get what they had struggled for over
many decades: the right to full citizenship. The so-called Justice Bell
helped them win the vote belatedly after the end of World War I.
Courtesy Liberty Bell Museum

While the Justice Bell was touring Pennsylvania in the summer of 1915, city officials prepared the Liberty Bell for its long journey. Since it was traveling to the West, where it had never been taken, they scheduled a circuitous route that would allow millions of Americans to see it for the first time. The long trip began conventionally with stops along the lines of the Pennsylvania Railroad through western Pennsylvania, Ohio, and Indiana to Chicago. Then, via the Chicago, Rock Island and Pacific Railway, the train snaked west, often stopping for five or ten minutes at towns with populations of only a few thousand in Illinois, Iowa, Kansas, and Nebraska. The train picked up the Union Pacific Railway to stop at Denver, then proceeded through Wyoming's vast ranchlands to Salt Lake City, Utah.

Stories abounded about the lengths to which people would go to gaze at the bell. A Wyoming cowgirl rode horseback for sixty miles to see the bell when it stopped at Cheyenne and Laramie; a Kansas boy walked barefoot for five miles to a town through which the train passed. In Colorado, the Centennial State, admitted to the union in 1876 on the hundredth anniversary of the Declaration of Independence, the bell had special appeal. The *Rocky Mountain News* gushed that "the desire to catch and keep something of the passing moment drew thousands as they filed by to stop a moment by the side of the car, to

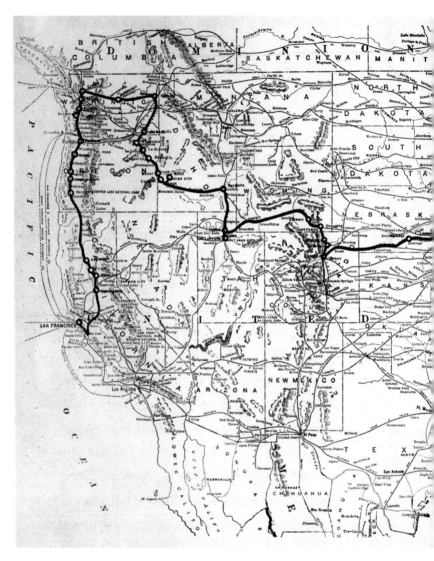

Map of Liberty Bell westward train journey in 1915. The Liberty Bell train passed through fifteen states and stopped at 64 towns and cities on the way from Philadelphia to San Francisco. On the return trip, on a

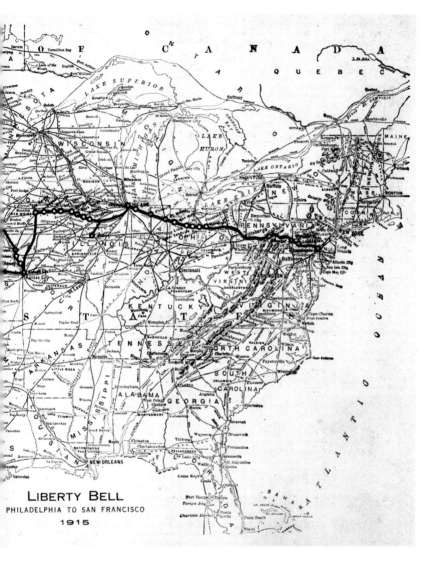

LIBERTY BELL
PHILADELPHIA TO SAN FRANCISCO
1915

southern route, it passed through fifteen states and made another
109 stops to accept the accolades of adoring Americans.
From the collection of Donna Ewald Huggins

stretch out to the guards a key, a coin, a bit of jewelry, a picture, any object that they had at hand, so that it might touch the old bell and then be treasured after the bell was gone. . . . Every other man, woman and child had a camera, anxious to get a picture of the occasion." For millions of westerners who could not visit San Francisco the Liberty Bell—its history and its meaning—became vivid and personal. In Denver, where the train pulled in as the sun rose and stopped for six hours, the entire metropolitan area mobbed it. "Out of the romantic memories of childhood's lessons," wrote a local newspaperman, "the school-bench history surrounded by the mystic spell of a nation's early struggle for life . . . the Liberty bell appeared to 140,000 persons in Denver . . . like the nucleus of an American idea."[43]

Rather than proceed directly to San Francisco, the bell train then headed farther north to Idaho, where it stopped at towns as small as Caldwell and Welser before chugging into Oregon. After five stops there along the coastal route, it steamed farther north through the state of Washington. Visits to Portland and Seattle were meant in part to compensate the Northwest for the refusal by the bell's keepers the previous decade to send it to the Lewis and Clark Centennial and American Pacific Exposition and Oriental Fair of 1905 and Seattle's Alaska-Yukon-Pacific Exposition in 1909. In Seattle the din of air horns and roaring crowds was nearly deafening, according to the *Seattle Post-Intelligencer.* At one point an elderly couple, struggling to get close, were hoisted up on the flatcar, where they kissed the bell, fell on their knees, and uttered a prayer. They bore "a radiant glow on their faces, indicating that one of the ambitions of their lives had been satisfied."[44]

Having sated the enthusiasm of hundreds of thousands in the Northwest, the bell train headed south on the Great Northern Railway, following the inland route to visit such California farming and ranching hamlets and towns as Red Bluff, Chico, Biggs, Marysville, and Lincoln, where it was met by "a patriotic outburst in the state unrivaled in times of peace." On its last lap to San Francisco, forty thousand people in Sacramento, California's capital but still only a small city of one hundred thousand, "stood for five hours in the sun in the hottest day of this year waiting for the Liberty Bell." Here, as at many of these stops, people came from great distances to glimpse the symbol of liberty that they had praised in song and read about in their schoolbooks. "It was as though the visible mantle of a national unity had been flung out over this part of the country," wrote a witness.[45]

By the time the bell neared San Francisco, some five million Americans had seen it on its way west. That was just a start. On July 16, 1915, a rapturous crowd turned out to welcome the Liberty Bell as it came across San

Train stop in Cayuse, Oregon, 1915. White men in straw boaters, Cayuse Indians and Chinese women in native dress, African Americans, and a reservation missionary all mingled near the Indian reservation to salute the Liberty Bell. From the collection of Donna Ewald Huggins

Francisco Bay. Workmen lifted it by crane onto a festooned motor truck, almost buried in roses. The next day was Liberty Bell Day, which brought an attendance of nearly 114,000. A massive parade, with flag-draped little girls representing the states of the Union and a juvenile Miss Columbia and Uncle Sam leading the way, carried the bell out to the Exposition's City of Ivory, built on the Bay between the Presidio and Fort Mason. Champ Clark, speaker of the House of Representatives, trying to push President Wilson out of his neutrality stance, thundered that "peace at any price is an amazing, a demoralizing, a degrading doctrine." In the shadow of the Liberty Bell, he argued that the government must maintain "at any cost every American right at home and abroad."[46]

Some had other reasons to celebrate the Liberty Bell. Among the visitors on July 30, 1915, was Billy Sunday, the golden-throated evangelist, who came "to aid in driving satan from the Western shore."[47]

Others came at the behest of corporate interests. Among them were two contingents of Blackfeet Indians, given an expenses-paid trip from the tribe's reservation near Browning, Montana, to San Francisco to promote the Great Northern Railroad and Glacier National Park. Arriving in a 1915 Packard that had participated in a St. Paul–to–San Francisco road race, they posed before the Liberty Bell, where Chief Little Bear, carefully instructed, placed his right hand on the bell while presenting the cameras with a stern countenance.

Had the Blackfeet really bought into the idea that the Liberty Bell was theirs as well? As thrilling as the Indians may have been to visitors, with their elaborate war bonnets, the Blackfeet men were a remnant of a once proud and numerous people who had been decimated by small-pox after they had hospitably sheltered the Lewis and Clark Expedition during Jefferson's presidency. By the late nineteenth century, the extermination of buffalo left

Blackfeet chiefs on way to San Francisco, 1915. Glacier National Park and the Great Northern Railway sponsored the Blackfoot chiefs' trip to San Francisco in 1915. The car was Glacier National Park's entry in the auto race from St. Paul, Minnesota, to San Francisco. From the collection of Donna Ewald Huggins

the Blackfeet facing starvation. Reduced to little more than a thousand in number, they had relinquished most of their remaining land to the federal government just five years before the Pan-Pacific Exposition. With this land cession, which made possible the creation of Glacier National Park, the 1855 tribal homeland of the Blackfeet had dwindled from 26 million acres to about 1.5 million. We cannot know what passed through the mind of Chief Little Bear as he placed his hand on the Liberty Bell and viewed the words "Proclaim Liberty throughout all the Land," but it is reasonable to guess that his posing before the bell at the Exposition was motivated less by the symbolism than the small financial benefits it brought to his desperately impoverished people.

For the next five months, the Liberty Bell was a must-see attraction. Even before the bell's arrival, visitors had had plenty of choices: the immense Canadian pavilion featuring a pond with a colony of beavers; Lincoln Beachey, the most famous aviator in the world, whose unbelievable stunt flying made him seem "death-proof," until his flying machine collapsed after a series of loops and rolls on March 14, killing him instantly; "Captain, the Educated Horse," who could add, subtract, match colors, and play songs on bells; and a five-acre reproduction of the Grand Canyon, complete with a village of Pueblo Indians.

But whatever else they saw, fairgoers *had* to see the Liberty Bell. The Exposition drew nearly nineteen million visitors—this matched the St. Louis Exposition record—and by one estimate, one-tenth of them kissed the Liberty Bell, even though it arrived in San Francisco five months after the festivities had begun. Many claimed the bell was the most photographed object at the Exposition.

Well it might have been, for it symbolized the nation's deepest values. Every night the bell was hustled into a special fireproof vault—a sure sign that it had become one of America's most treasured objects. Such precautions were taken after a report circulated that a stick of dynamite had been hurled at the bell.[48]

After the Liberty Bell left San Francisco on November 11, the historian of the Exposition rhapsodized: "Who shall say that the journey of the great national relic through the breadth of the national territory and back did not have a very large share in uniting and stiffening the public resolution to defend that Nation's rights when the fiery test came?"[49] Just as the Panama-Pacific Exposition induced spectacular touristic consumption, it also spurred spectacular American patriotism, all the more so because the lights were going out all over Europe.

Before the Liberty Bell returned to Philadelphia, it had one more errand to fulfill. San Diego was also holding an exposition—the Panama-California International Exposition—in late 1915, but San Diego had lost out to San Francisco as the Liberty Bell's summer home on the Pacific Slope. In fact, San Diego officials were able to call their exposition international only after half a dozen European nations had their exhibits shipped south after the San Francisco Expo ended. But at least Philadelphia officials had allowed the bell to delay its homecoming for the sake of a long, sweeping southward odyssey down the agricultural San Joaquin Valley, stopping at small, dusty farming towns such as Fresno, Porterville, and Bakersfield, and culminating in three days in San Diego.

By the time it reached San Diego, the Liberty Bell had stopped at 169 towns and cities since leaving Philadelphia on its transcontinental trip. San Diego's officials made the most of the bell's final visit on the West Coast, scheduling Liberty Bell Day for November 12. San Diego was still a city of only about fifty-five thousand, and the turnouts were naturally much smaller than in San Francisco. But the crowds were just as Liberty Bell–crazy as elsewhere in the nation. At 8:30 A.M. all church and school bells rang for five minutes, while boat and factory whistles joined in. Admitted free to the exposition grounds, some fourteen thousand schoolchildren poured into the Plaza de Panama, heaped garlands of flowers on "the best jewel of American historical relics," and sang "The Star-Spangled Banner." "Tears stood in the eyes of many who had been brought up on the legend of the bell," wrote the *San Diego Union*. "The spell of history was on them."[50]

Leaving San Diego at midnight on November 15, 1915, the Liberty Bell started its long journey home, again on a circuitous, whistle-stop route that brought another five million people out to see it. After a seven-hour stop in Los Angeles, it headed through Arizona and New Mexico

Return trip from San Francisco to Philadelphia. From the collection of
Donna Ewald Huggins

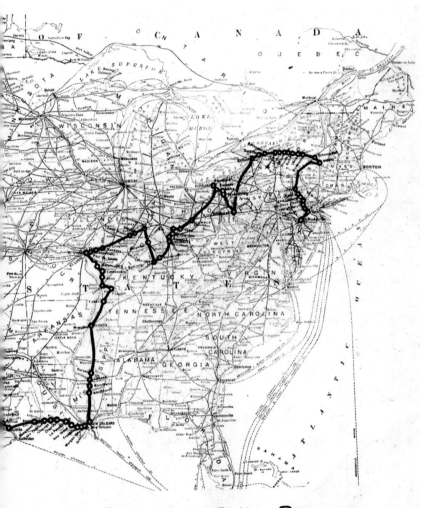

CAL. TO PHILADELPHIA PA.

to Texas. Sometimes the train stopped for five or ten minutes at small towns, often in the wee hours of morning. Even at such places as San Simon, Arizona; Marfa, Corsicana, and Navasota, Texas; and New Iberia, Louisiana, a human sea of store clerks, mechanics, pensioners, ranchers, oil riggers, and townspeople of every description rose at all hours of night when the train was scheduled to stop at their town. If they sensed that this might be their last chance to see the revered bell and to experience the magical moment of touching or kissing it, they were right.

Rather than proceeding directly from Texas to Philadelphia, the bell train was routed northward from Louisiana through Tennessee and Kentucky to Illinois, then eastward through Indiana and Ohio. Onward to Pittsburgh, the bell train swung in a northeastern arc to upstate New York before winding southward through Pennsylvania's coalfields, the Pocono Mountains, and then finally into New Jersey before returning to Pennsylvania. On November 25 the train swept into Philadelphia, way behind schedule and long after dark. The next morning, Philadelphians turned out en masse to welcome their beloved bell home after its ten thousand–mile trip through thirty states. Frenzies of patriotism erupted as Philadelphians poured out their emotions. Little ones astride their fathers' shoulders, babies raised high, cheering crowds and an exuberant press corps filled the morning newspapers about the great homecoming.[51]

Never again would the Liberty Bell leave the city. Its fame would grow, but its mobility now was strictly limited. The bell had accepted the laurels of an entire generation of Americans, and the nation's schoolchildren had been taught—in poems, songs, and schoolbook stories—to revere the bell. These were the Americans who would carry their devotion to the Liberty Bell as the sentinel of freedom into two world wars.

FOUR

The Liberty Bell in War and Peace

After the United States entered the Great War on April 2, 1917, the Liberty Bell was enlisted, along with 9.5 million men, to make the world safe for democracy. To raise the money to support the war, President Woodrow Wilson and Congress authorized Liberty Bonds to "beat back the Hun." Naturally, the Liberty Bell was appointed chief salesman of the bonds by which the American public would lend money to their government to conduct the war. "Old Liberty Bell to Peal for Bonds," announced a *New York Times* headline the day before Flag Day in 1917, the reporter noting, "Its peals will call America to defend her traditions."[1] Warned by metallurgists at Philadelphia's Franklin Institute that the unstable bell could not withstand the strike of its clapper, city officials settled for tapping the bell at noon on June 14 to launch the loan drive. Four months later, workmen hoisted the bell on top of a float for a gala Liberty Loan parade. The hope that this would drum up millions of dollars of subscriptions was more than realized: Americans oversubscribed the loan drive by $500 million.

From that point on, the Liberty Bell was a stand-in for the American defense of democracy in Europe. Marshal Joseph Joffre, to be called "the savior of France," hastened across the Atlantic to Philadelphia to kiss the Liberty Bell and make appropriate speeches to pump up American war patriotism. Right behind him were the heralded French "Blue Devils." Decorated for bravery on the western front, Les Diables Bleus arrived in their distinctive blue uniforms with flowing capes and jaunty berets to tour the country and spur the sale of Liberty Bonds. They thrilled Philadelphians when they "showered the bell with kisses of adulation," and "so great was their joy," reported the *Public Ledger*, that "some of the party tenderly placed their arms about the bell and hugged it, just as a southern 'mammy' caresses one of her 'chilluns.'" Newspapers whipped up emotions to a bond-buying froth by imagining what would happen "if the Kaiser and his vandals came to Philadelphia." After torching the University of Pennsylvania (as they did the University of Louvain), despoiling the Betsy Ross House, bombing Independence

Hall, and shredding the Declaration of Independence, the "minions of frightfulness" would then eye the Liberty Bell. "The Liberty Bell! Imagine the Crown Prince tapping it ruthlessly with his riding whip while twisting his dainty mustache and saying to Ludendorff, 'Just a few more machine gun bullets, Ludy, old boy, until we get to Pittsburgh and the Ozark Mountains.' Whereupon the grand old Liberty Bell would go the way of all the fine old bronzed bells of Belgium and France into the Hun melting pot."[2]

Philadelphia was one of the many cities that held Liberty Bell days, but the Quaker City's day to sell bonds was hands-down the most memorable. On October 24, 1917, "The great demonstration formed a living shrine for the Liberty Bell," reported a Philadelphia newspaper. Veterans from service dating back to the Civil War donned old uniforms to march in a massive parade led by the Liberty Bell, which was mounted on a motor truck with its supports and yoke draped with flags and flowers. When the truck reached the Liberty Loan headquarters, it "became the center of a vast sea of faces while 'America' and 'The Star Spangled Banner,' sung by the assembled multitude, rose in a mighty volume of sound as a tribute to the emblem of freedom hanging silent in their midst."[3] Two more such drives ensued, with the Liberty Bell the star symbol of patriotic sacrifice. Masses of miniature liberty

Twenty-five thousand soldiers gathered at Fort Dix, New Jersey, in 1918 to form "The Human Liberty Bell" to promote Liberty Bell Bonds and whip up patriotism for a war that was far from popular. Courtesy Independence National Historical Park

bells were given out to subscribers, and true patriots displayed Liberty Bell stickers in their front windows with the words "We Have Rung It Again." Americans oversubscribed the five billion dollars of Liberty Bonds this time.

The Liberty Bell, if not the original then its replica,

also went overseas to promote the war against the Axis powers. Immigrants from the old Hapsburg Empire, forming the Mid-European Union, met in Independence Hall only weeks before the armistice. There they promulgated a declaration of independence in "defiance against autocracy, aristocracy, and imperialism" and began the process of hammering out structures for free governments after the war. Tomas G. Masaryk, president of the Union, read the Declaration of Independence from the steps of America's birthplace.

What could better symbolize these efforts than a new Liberty Bell? Commissioned to cast a large replica of the Liberty Bell was the Meneely Bell Company of Troy, New York, which had cast the Seybert Bell, the Centennial Bell, the Columbian Bell, and the Suffrage Bell. Soon the bell was taken to Czechoslovakia, where in 1928 it rang in the tenth anniversary of the nation's independence in Prague.[4] Thought to have disappeared during World War II—metal-hungry German forces were said to have melted it down, intent on hurling it back at the Allied forces in the form of bombs and bullets—it was found hidden away in the Prague Castle and rehung in the 1980s in the left tower of St. Anthony's Church.[5]

Armistice Day, November 11, 1918, brought a gigantic crowd to Independence Hall. With visitors still able to touch and kiss the bell, an estimated sixty thousand to seventy thousand streamed through the first floor of Independence Hall to pay their respects to the precious relic. Once more, the Liberty Bell was taken for a stroll along Chestnut Street on May 15, 1919, to welcome home the Doughboys from "Over There."[6]

But patriotism waned as Americans rolled into the 1920s to revel in flapper girls, jazz, and the new era of radio and movies. In 1922, looking for the kind of commercial bounty that had flowed from the Columbian Exposition of 1893, Chicago planned its Second Annual Pageant of Progress. Chicago officials topped all previous attempts at gathering children's signatures for a monster petition—this time 3.4 million tots signed on—and argued, "Never before in the history of the United States has the patriotism of the American people been so feeble. The country needs to see the bell to rekindle their patriotism." But Philadelphia officials turned Chicago down. The mayor argued that Philadelphia's main task now was to protect the bell and spare it any further wear and tear on the road. In 1939 city officials held their ground and disappointed New York World's Fair commissioners, who had to content themselves with a replica of the bell and a Japanese version composed of 11,600 pearls, 366 diamonds, and 26 pounds of silver.[7]

So the Liberty Bell rested. Soon ahead was the sesquicentennial of the Declaration of Independence in 1926.

General John "Blackjack" Pershing at the Liberty Bell, 1919.
Courtesy Independence National Historical Park

Despite great hopes of Philadelphia leaders that this would be another commercial bonanza, shoddy planning and terrible weather turned it into a bust. But at least the Liberty Bell Fair, as it was called, occasioned a tidal wave of souvenirs, postcards, guidebooks, and assorted apparel.

And if the tourists didn't come, several million tuned in on radio, now in nearly every household, to listen to the sound of the mayor's wife tap out in Morse code "1926" on the Liberty Bell with a rubber-tipped hammer. Obligingly, for the first time in American history the U.S. Post Office Department issued a commemorative postage stamp of the Liberty Bell with a print run of 307,731,900 copies that ensured it would appear on letters for years to come.

Those who did attend the fairgrounds in South Philadelphia did not see the Liberty Bell because the city council heeded arguments that the bell was too fragile for further excursions and, as the superintendent of Independence Hall spouted, "one might as well take the Declaration Table or any other cherished relic of that incomparable Shrine and cart it around for exhibition purposes." But at least exposition-goers were shown a colossal replica of the Liberty Bell. It towered eighty feet above South Broad Street and was illuminated by twenty-six thousand electric light bulbs. If "inflated to absurd proportions," as one historian has commented, the Liberty Bell was keeping step with the latest technological gimmicks.[8]

As the Roaring Twenties progressed, the Liberty Bell and Independence Hall began to occupy different places in the American consciousness. Independence Hall was a place and a physical landmark. It could not escape its neighborhood, which by the 1920s was becoming a seedy commercial area crowded with eastern European immigrants. Better days were still ahead, but for now it receded as a decaying national monument. The Liberty Bell, on the other hand, was a symbol, indeed an international symbol, etched into the minds of nearly every American and countless others abroad. Thirty years of traveling—of being photographed, touched, kissed, and caressed—had enhanced its reputation as the bell that belonged to everybody. Moreover, the marketing of its image in millions of trinkets, postcards, miniature versions, and memorabilia, and its role in the World War I war bond effort, had made it the indispensable American icon. On New Year's Eve in 1924, 1925, and 1926, it was the tapping of the Liberty Bell, broadcast by radio across the nation, that welcomed in the New Year. By the end of the 1920s, there was hardly a sensate person in America who did not know about the Liberty Bell, and those who did not treasure it were rare.

In case there was someone still not cognizant of the Liberty Bell's significance, further tappings of the bell continued as the nation struggled through the Great Depression. No rich tone could be coaxed from the bell with a wooden or rubber-tipped mallet, but Americans got accustomed to the dull thud, thud, thud and thought no less of their beloved Liberty Bell. In January 1931 the bell was tapped to celebrate the 225th anniversary of the birth of Benjamin Franklin; later that year to celebrate the 200th anniversary of George Washington's birth; and on July 4, 1934, when Rear Admiral Richard E. Byrd, standing in Antarctica, transmitted a radio signal that through electronic impulse caused the rubber-tipped hammer to gently strike the bell. July 4, 1935, brought another national broadcast of the bell-tapping, by now a regular routine. The tapping stepped up in 1937: to commemorate the Constitutional Convention of 1787 (with a tapper made from a dogwood tree at Valley Forge carried to Independence Hall by a relay team of Boy Scouts); and another thirteen times on October 15, 1937, to open the Second Annual National Negro Congress—thirteen taps in honor of the Thirteenth Amendment, which ended slavery in the United States.[9]

While the fame of the Liberty Bell grew and grew, Independence Hall began to lose its place as a public arena for contestation and commemoration. Even before World War I, the city had passed an ordinance limiting the use of Independence Square for political gatherings, following the request in 1912 from the Industrial Workers of the World to gather in front of Independence Hall. The IWW was feared by many Americans as a radical and violent organization led by European immigrant anarchists, and city officials certainly shared this view. Therefore, they banned all assemblages except for "patriotic meetings to celebrate some event in the history of the Nation, State, or City."

Visitors were as free as ever to enter Independence Hall and see the Liberty Bell. They did so every year by tens of thousands. But no longer could anyone come to promote a cause. Even when coming simply to gaze at the Liberty Bell, guests found new restrictions. Trying to limit the commercial exploitation of the nation's most celebrated artifact, Philadelphia officials shuttered the cameras. "I am getting tired of taking pictures of chorus girls, chewing-gum promoters, and the like standing beside the bell," the city's chief of property groaned. From now on, a city permit was needed to snap a picture.[10]

While putting Independence Hall out of bounds to political organizers and demonstrators, city officials could do nothing to prevent organizations of every political stripe to make what they would of the bell. In Michigan the Independent Progressive Party, a remnant of the Progressive Movement that had fizzled out after World War I, unveiled the Liberty Bell Ringers in September 1924 to keep alive some of the unrealized Progressive reforms. Traveling the country, the bell ringers drummed up votes for their presidential candidate while pushing legislation to complete the Progressive agenda. A month later, a citizens group formed the Loyal Fraternity of the Liberty

Bell to fight the resurgent Ku Klux Klan's attempts to gain a foothold in the federal Veterans' Bureau.[11] Others, thinking the Liberty Bell mantle might protect them when they practiced their brand of freedom, had no such good fortune. Acting under the provisions of the Eighteenth Amendment, prohibiting the production or sale of spiritous beverages, federal agents descended on the Liberty Bell Brewing Company in Paterson, New Jersey, in January 1925, seized $10,000 worth of equipment, and dumped twenty-five thousand gallons of beer outside the plant.[12]

With Europe tottering on the precipice of war by 1936, at a time when isolationism in the United States was strong but so was fear of the rise of fascism in Europe, the Liberty Bell became the emblem for diametrically opposed organizations. The American Friends Service Committee, the most important pacifist organization in the United States, convinced Philadelphia officials to tap the Liberty Bell in a broadcast that reached across the nation and throughout Europe as part of their Emergency Peace Campaign. But a few months later, Philadelphia's mayor tapped the bell at the Democratic National Convention and speechified that Americans must "breathe in again, tonight, the spirit of this historic bell; [and] rededicate ourselves to eternal warfare against all enemies of our government." The Liberty Bell recognized no particular political party, so it was altogether appropriate that it was tapped thirteen times in June 1940 to mark the opening of the Republican National Convention and then again in August for the Democratic Party.[13]

The Great Depression dampened tourist traffic at Independence Hall, just as it cast a pall over almost everything else in the stricken United States. But that changed with the advent of World War II. Even before the United States entered the war, the bell's millions of admirers were primed to imagine how it would save the entire world. The city's best-selling morning newspaper, the *Philadelphia Inquirer*, described a hypothetical invasion of the United States by Germany, thwarted by the capture of Hitler. The evil Nazi leader would be brought to Philadelphia to sign the Third Reich's surrender in front of the Liberty Bell. "Proclaim Liberty throughout all the Land" (and throughout the world) would once more be heard, even if figuratively, from the ancient icon.[14]

But beyond fantasy lurked reality. With Germany blitzkrieging its way through Europe, and President Franklin D. Roosevelt trying to wean his nation from isolationism, the nation began to mobilize for war. Uncle Sam pointed his finger at the American public, saying, "I Want You," to stir up military enlistments; but it was the Liberty Bell that the government wheeled out again to sell the Treasury Department War Bonds. The image of the

Revolutionary War Minuteman, redolent of the soldier-citizens at Concord Bridge in April 1775, edged out the Liberty Bell as the image on the stamps that millions of Americans purchased at their local post offices and pasted into War Savings Books (to be redeemed in cash at the end of the war). But the bell was featured prominently on the posters and advertisements that powered seven War Bond drives to finance the war. When Roosevelt and Congress ordered a national lottery in October 1940 for the first peacetime draft in United States history, the first Philadelphians inducted into the armed service took their oath of enlistment before the Liberty Bell. As the familiar symbol of American determination to defend liberty in Europe, the Liberty Bell reported for duty on recruiting posters and many other "support-the-war" media, including military training films.[15]

Children also had to be enlisted in the war effort for scrap metal drives and newspaper drives—and if the war lasted for long, they would themselves be called to the battle lines. Gas rationing meant that orange school buses could no longer bring children to see the Liberty Bell. But *Old Liberty Bell* filled the gap. Written by Frances Rogers and Alice Beard, authors of such historically themed children's books as *Big Miss Liberty*, *The Birthday of a Nation*, and *Paul Revere*, *Old Liberty Bell* reached school libraries all over the country in 1942. "This is the story of a bell with the gift of prophecy," the authors began. On the next page, youngsters read,

> For many years we looked upon the [Liberty Bell] as a cherished relic of the past. Freedom was already won, forever established throughout many a land besides our own—or so we believed. No need for any further proclamation of liberty. We came to regard the Bell as an erstwhile prophet who spoke only of yesterday, not of tomorrow.
>
> Then suddenly, in the middle of the twentieth century, we were undeceived.
>
> Again we must fight for freedom as we did in '76. But this time standing proudly shoulder to shoulder with England and with all nations—the United Nations—who value freedom above life.[16]

While raising money and recruiting sailors, soldiers, marines, and fliers, the Liberty Bell had to be protected. Shocked by Pearl Harbor, Americans feared that secret enemy agents would try to sap American morale by destroying their sacred relic. Some suggested that the Liberty Bell should be sent south under cloak of night to wait out the war far beneath the surface at Fort Knox. Others preferred digging a deep shaft under Independence Hall, where the bell could be surrounded by thirty-two hundred pounds of steel and lowered by elevator in case of an air raid or furtive attack. This solution was abandoned for fear that digging a bomb shelter would compromise the integrity of Independence Hall, and the federal War Production Board declined to contribute to this effort. Moving less dramatically, officials doubled and redoubled the guards at Independence Hall and enhanced fire protection measures. At the same time, they positioned the bell on a platform with rubber-wheeled tires so that practiced guards could whisk it out of Independence Hall should the venerable building come under attack.[17]

Eternal vigilance had its price. Trying to enforce the earlier decision to require a city permit in order to photograph the Liberty Bell, guards arrested a *Philadelphia Record* reporter on July 3, 1942, for snapping his camera. "I was arrested yesterday," wrote Joseph Shallit. "My crime was to try to take a snapshot of the Liberty Bell. In this birthplace of American liberty, in the year of our independence, the 166th, a citizen isn't permitted to photograph the bell that once proclaimed 'liberty throughout all the land unto all the inhabitants thereof.'" After Shallit protested that no law prohibited his photography, the city police asked him, "Are you a Communist?" and told him he could be sent up for ten years. The police threw him in a cell with a drunk to await a hearing. The case was dismissed, but wartime jitters continued, while the

the war. Glued to their radios, millions of Americans heard the Liberty Bell tap out VICTORY.[20]

To what extent the several million Americans who served in World War II carried the mental image of the Liberty Bell into battle cannot be determined, but hardly any of them were unaware that it was the nation's sentinel of freedom. Obviously this was in the mind of the airmen who christened their B-17 Flying Fortress *Liberty Belle* near the end of the war. Attached to the 390th Bomber Group, the plane was part of the sortie that attacked Düsseldorf, Germany, with disastrous results for the airmen. *Liberty Belle* was one of the few that returned to home base. After that, it completed sixty-four combat missions. Bearing the insignia of a shapely redhead in Gibson Girl attire extending her arm over Philadelphia's Liberty Bell, the Flying Fortress ended up in the Virgil "Gus" Grissom Air Museum in Peru, Indiana. When school groups tour the museum today and ask why Miss Belle is topless, tour guides explain that the wind is so strong up there where the plane flies that her blouse simply blew off. (Today, another B-17, restored to its World War II glory and called the *Liberty Belle*, takes you aloft for a thirty-minute nostalgic flight for $460 per person. One of fourteen B-17s still in the air, it barnstorms the country as the prized possession—and cash cow—of the Liberty Foundation of Tulsa, Oklahoma.)[21]

Other airmen climbed into a B-24 Liberator also named *Liberty Belle* but known familiarly to the airmen as the "Strawberry Bitch." Part of the 450th Heavy Bombardment Group, flying from its base in southern Italy, the plane carried the image of a bare-breasted, long-legged morale-boosting brunette with a winsome smile.[22]

The U.S. Navy did not miss out, either, on the Liberty Bell cachet. Acquiring an old 622-ton rust-bucket built in 1910 for service at the Naval Mine Warfare Test Station in Solomons, Maryland, the navy named it the *Liberty Bell*. And from the shipyards in Oakland, California, the Kaiser Shipbuilding Company, the parent of Kaiser Medical group, turned out Liberty Ships at the rate of one per day.

The Liberty Bell might have rested with the Allied victory over Germany and Japan in late 1945 had not the Cold War ensued. But the USSR-U.S. confrontation guaranteed otherwise. Most of the headlines featured military and diplomatic maneuvering as the two superpowers crossed swords. But the cultural war, like a play within a play, concerned the American way of life. Defending democracy and convincing Third World nations emerging from the domination of colonial European masters that the road forward was alignment with the democratic, capitalist West rather than with the Communist, collectivist Soviet Union required "a clearly articulated message about the nation's principles." The Liberty Bell and its landlord, Independence Hall, became signal parts of the message.[23]

Showing unity and rock-ribbed strength at home, demonstrating that Americans were as faithful to their beliefs and values as medieval monks on a pilgrimage, was critically important to Cold Warriors. Senator Joseph McCarthy's crusade to purge the government of Communists and Communist sympathizers was one expression of this impulse. Another was manifest in displays of old-fashioned American patriotism, verging on xenophobia. John Stormer, the fiery anti-Communist organizer and author of the best-selling *None Dare Call It Treason*, proudly launched Liberty Bell Press in 1963. The press still purveys propaganda from the extreme right of the political spectrum. Another ultraconservative group, now defunct, adopted the name Liberty Bell Publications.

In this culture war, Independence Hall and the Liberty Bell became the indispensable symbols of the American way. The proposal for a Loyalty Day in 1949 by the Veterans of Foreign Wars, endorsed by Congress, produced an annual parade that ended at Independence Hall in a boisterous celebration of American values, American unity, and American strength. Seen as an antidote to the internationally celebrated May Day (also known as International Workers Day or Labour Day), with its working-class, even socialist, tincture, Loyalty Day in 1950 attracted some five million Americans in rallies held across the nation. In Philadelphia, the Catholic War Veterans, Jewish War Veterans, American Legion, and Veterans of Foreign Wars, led by high school bands and throngs of schoolchildren, marched shoulder to shoulder. Helped along by cheap gasoline and the postwar enthusiasm for automobile vacations, Americans began making pilgrimages to Philadelphia. Visitors to Independence Hall and its iconic tenant more than doubled after 1950, exceeding a million by 1957.

The federal government left no stone unturned in trying to use the Liberty Bell as the beacon demonstrating American unity and strength. In 1950, the same year that Loyalty Day came into existence, the Department of the Treasury, in cooperation with several private corporations, commissioned a French foundry to cast fifty-four full-size replicas of the Liberty Bell to be given to each state and territory of the United States and the District of Columbia. Ford Motor Company did its patriotic (and profitable) part by providing red, white, and blue trucks to carry the bells to each state capital. To be rung on patriotic occasions, the replicas would keep the Liberty Bell in everyone's mind as the nation's great sentinel of freedom. Most repose today at state capitol buildings or grounds, but some are found in places as varied as the Old Arsenal Museum in Louisiana, St. John's College in Annapolis, Maryland, and the town square in Perth Amboy, New Jersey. Wisconsin officials placed their bell at the Girls' Detention Center, but later moved it to a public park in Sheboygan and then to the capitol building in Madison after worries arose that the delinquent girls might proclaim their own liberty by scaling the prison walls.

Exporting the Liberty Bell message became an important part of Washington's Cold War cultural strategy to stifle Communism. For example, the federal government sent full-size replicas of the bell to Israel in 1950 to recognize the birth of the state of Israel. Another replica went to Japan in 1951 as part of the program to sway Japanese voters from electing a Socialist government.[24] The Treasury Department again called on the ever-dutiful Liberty Bell in 1950 to help sell savings bonds in a so-called Independence Drive. But independence and freedom had taken on a new meaning: the might of the Soviet Union extended over all of Eastern Europe, its threat over all the world. The bond drive, announced President Truman's vice president, Alben W. Barkley, was to make America "so strong no one can impose ruthless, godless ideologies on us."[25]

A gigantic replica of the Liberty Bell resonated with especially ringing tones in West Berlin as part of a Cold

War tactic carefully planned by the CIA. A ten-ton knock-off of the original was installed in the two hundred–foot tower of the Rathaus Schöneberg, West Berlin's city hall, on United Nations Day, October 24, 1950. It differed from the Liberty Bell in some respects: a laurel wreath symbolizing peace encircled the top and five figures representing the five (presumed) races of humankind were shown on a frieze with outstretched arms holding torches of freedom. An added inscription used Abraham Lincoln's words at Gettysburg: "That this world under God shall have a new birth of freedom."

The Berlin Liberty Bell, officially called the World Freedom Bell, had been commissioned by the Crusade for Freedom campaign, sponsored by the National Committee for a Free Europe, the CIA-directed group operating Radio Free Europe. Cast in England, the bell was first shipped to the United States, where it received a ticker-tape parade down Fifth Avenue in New York City. Building toward the Berlin climax, it then visited twenty-one American cities, where sixteen million Americans signed a Declaration of Freedom pledging their belief "that all men derive the right to freedom equally from God"—the Declaration of Independence made no such claim for God as the dispenser of freedom—and would "resist aggression and tyranny wherever they appear on earth." From New York, it crossed the Atlantic to Bremerhaven,

Germany, and then traveled by covered railroad flatcar to Berlin.

Some four hundred thousand Berliners—perhaps one hundred thousand risked crossing from East Berlin—poured into the square to witness the dedication ceremonies. General Lucius D. Clay, former U.S. military governor of Germany and becoming famous as the "father of the Berlin airlift" of 1948–49, gave the speech—timed to end just before high noon—about the "free world's determination to resist Communist aggression." According to U.S. government accounts, the overcast skies "suddenly cleared and bright sunshine flooded the vast square" as Clay pushed the button exactly at noon that started the clapper ringing the bell.

Its pealing could be heard throughout the city and well into East Berlin, just as intended. Simultaneously, the Voice of America and Radio Free Europe, in the "widest broadcast hookup ever attempted by radio," blanketed Eastern Europe with the ringing of the bell. Not impressed, Hans Jendretsky, Politburo member of the German Democratic Republic in East Germany, warned "the rope of the death bell will become the gallows rope for those who ring it." Of course, this did not stop the Freedom Bell from ringing on Sundays just before noon, at midnight on Christmas Eve, and on New Year's Eve—

Freedom Bell
Tolls Message
Of Hope and Faith

By LOWELL BENNETT
*Chief, Public Relations Branch,
HICOG-Berlin Element*

THE DEEP BRONZE TONES of the World Freedom Bell pealed out a message of hope and of faith from Berlin's City Hall tower at high noon on Oct. 24. Nearly half a million Berliners, massed in the vast square below, and millions of radio listeners throughout the world, heard the great bell toll and knew this was the symbolic call for a global crusade for freedom.

It was an inspiring tribute to this city's stalwart stand against the unceasing pressures of Communism. And it was an impressive climax to the growing determination of free men everywhere to destroy the evil roots of oppression and terror.

Gen. Lucius Dr. Clay, former US military governor of Germany and now national chairman of the Crusade for Freedom, returned to Berlin on that day to dedicate the bell. Flanking him at the City Hall ceremony were John J. McCloy, US high commissioner for Germany, Maj. Gen. Maxwell D. Taylor, US commander of Berlin, and Prof. Ernst Reuter, mayor of Greater Berlin. With them was a galaxy of leading political and diplomatic representatives from 30 nations, gathered together for the ceremony on a free island 105 miles behind the Iron Curtain.

It had been shipped across the Atlantic to Bremerhaven on the naval transport "General Blatchford" — a freedom ship which had carried 13,833 refugees and displaced persons from Europe to sanctuary in the United States — and brought on a covered railroad flat-car to Berlin. With it came "freedom scrolls" which bore the signatures of millions of Americans from all walks of life, men and women who signed the declaration of freedom:

"I believe in the sacredness and dignity of the individual;

Berliners (above) register determination for freedom as crowd estimated at 500,000 (below) turns out for dedication ceremony.

Liberty Bell replica in Berlin, 1950. The newsletter of the High Commission for Germany published this photo of half a million Berliners turning out for a Cold War extravaganza in 1950. The article's headline was "Freedom Bell Tolls Message of Hope and Faith." From Lowell Bennett, "Freedom Bell," *Information Bulletin* (Frankfurt, Germany: Office of the U.S. High Commissioner for Germany Office of Public Affairs, Public Relations Division, 1950), [48–50] always heard over Radio Free Europe behind the Iron Curtain.[26]

Nobody in the Cold War crusade against Communism figured out a way to outdo the deployment of the Liberty Bell replica in West Berlin, for who could have dared to predict such an atmospheric parting of the clouds at the very moment the bell began to peal? Yet attempts to harvest the Liberty Bell bounty continued. The Liberty Bell figured prominently in the space race with the Soviet Union during the 1960s. *Liberty Bell* 7, a space capsule manned by U.S. Air Force Captain Virgil "Gus" Grissom, spent fifteen minutes in space in 1961—this was the second American suborbital space flight—before Grissom splashed down in the Atlantic Ocean off the coast of Florida. Meant to become a symbol of hope of catching up with the Soviet Union, the *Liberty Bell* 7 remained three hundred feet underwater for thirty-eight years before a Discovery Channel expedition recovered it in 2000 and painstakingly restored it.

The use of the Liberty Bell as a weapon in the West's Cold War arsenal continued for several decades. When Philadelphia officials refused to send the bell to the 1958 Brussels World's Fair, a whiskey company paid to have a one-third-size replica cast and delivered to the fair. The bell would serve "as an unbeatable weapon in United States propaganda against the Russians," wrote the *Observer.* "As a symbol of freedom and the rights of man—it's a symbol no Communist can hope to beat."[27]

The Liberty Bell could not stop the building of the Berlin Wall in 1961, but it became the custom to tap the bell mournfully over the radio each year to lament the construction of this Cold War antisymbol of freedom. What effect these broadcasts had as they circled the world is hard to determine. But the immense Freedom Bell in West Berlin was rung to honor such events as the Hungarian uprising of 1956 and the reunification of Germany in 1990.

In the Asian theater of the Cold War, the Liberty Bell also came into play. Between 1950 and 1953 the Korean War inflamed much of Asia and cost several hundred thousand casualties. Once a truce had been called and the United Nations charged a military armistice commission with keeping the peace, one of the strategic points in the demilitarized zone between North Korea and South Korea was named Camp Liberty Bell. Years later, in August 1976, North Korean troops attacked the camp and inflicted several casualties. Today, thousands of visitors tour the area annually.

While the Liberty Bell was symbolically fighting the Cold War in Europe and Asia from its perch in the corridor of Independence Hall, overseas Cold Warriors flocked to Philadelphia to visit the bell. It was nothing new for foreign dignitaries to pay respects to the cracked national icon. In 1930, for example, Washington Luis Pereira de Sousa, the last president of Brazil's First Republic, had posed in front of the bell after receiving an honorary degree from the University of Pennsylvania. Six years later, Cardinal Pacelli, the papal secretary of state and soon to become Pope Pius XII, stopped by as part of a whirlwind tour of the United States.[28]

The post–World War II roster of visitors, however, grew longer and longer, spurred by the Liberty Bell's significance as an international symbol of anti-Communism energetically promoted by the State Department. Albert Tarchiani, the Italian ambassador, laid a wreath before the Old Bell in early 1948. Ernst Reuter, mayor of West Berlin, arrived in 1951, only months after the Freedom Bell had taken his city by storm, to lay a wreath at the foot of the bell. Premier Mohammed Mossedeq of Iran, soon to be muscled out of office by the CIA, visited to pay his respects, as did Prime Minister David Ben-Gurion of Israel. Clement Attlee, prime minister of England, came the next year; Nicholas Kallay, premier of Hungary, paid his respects in March 1955; Mario Scelba, premier of Italy, came the next month; Abba Eban, the Israeli ambassador, came to associate Israel's ninth Independence Day with the bell's call to "Proclaim Liberty throughout all the Land"; and a later mayor of West Berlin, Willy

Brandt, came in 1958 to cement the city's good relations with the United States by bowing before the bell.

By this time, it was almost obligatory for an overseas diplomat or head of state to make a side trip from Washington, DC, where his main business was to be done, to affirm his reverence for the Liberty Bell. The bell was also on the agenda of Third World nations gaining their independence. The Ghanaian delegation that visited the bell on March 6, 1957, was one of many emerging nations that looked on the Liberty Bell as a talisman of national liberation from a century or more of European colonialism.

At the rare moments of thaw in Soviet-U.S. relations, it was natural that the Liberty Bell would be at the center of the action. When twelve Soviet officials visited Independence Hall in February 1960, they had to overcome hecklers shouting "Red murderers" and "You can't fool us."[29] Handshakes and insults were traded in a standoff. But in a later decade, after the Berlin Wall came down and the Cold War ended, Russian visitors got a kinder reception.

While the Liberty Bell played its part in the Cold War by hosting dignitary friends, it was also claimed as an inspiriting symbol by various groups at home. Convinced that the federal income tax, established by the Sixteenth Amendment in 1913, was unconstitutional, a national crusade of women formed the Liberty Belles in 1951 to carry their message around the nation.[30] More contested than using the image this way outside Philadelphia was staging demonstrations at Independence Square, with the Liberty Bell as the focal point. The city ordinance against using such "sacred ground," except for patriotic commemorations of the past, was intended to sanitize and control this piece of very public land. But after World War II, many groups across the political spectrum were eager to show that Independence Hall and the Liberty Bell were "not simply a mirror of the past, but a place where the nation could be challenged and redefined."[31]

One poignant example of this was the mission of Richard Robert Wright Sr., who had been born in slavery. Even while World War II raged, Wright had proposed a National Freedom Day to commemorate Lincoln's signing of the legislation that led to the Thirteenth Amendment. In this way, Americans would be reminded that the distance between the nation's ideals and realities was still vast. Wright first laid a wreath at the Liberty Bell on February 1, 1942, but not until the 1950s did this commemoration begin to attract wide notice. Wright's success in establishing National Freedom Day added an exclamation point to what by now had become a unique attribute of the Liberty Bell: that venerating it was a way of celebrating past accomplishments in the name of freedom, but that wreath-laying at its foot was even more important in pointing to the nation's uncompleted agenda.

After the war, public debate sparked challenges to the city's old restriction on political gatherings in Independence Square, where the Liberty Bell sedately rested. With McCarthyism raging and ten Hollywood writers being fingered for suspected Communist leanings, the Progressive Citizens of America went to court for the right to hold a rally in Independence Square. A federal judge overruled the city's refusal of permission. The meeting drew plenty of supporters, as well as counterdemonstrators shouting "Back to Russia!" But a First Amendment principle had been laid down. The use of the environs of the Liberty Bell, and all of Independence Square, now seemed to be available to all. Still straining to restrict First Amendment rights, the city passed a new ordinance permitting political activities only on sixteen specified days.[32]

After the Supreme Court ruled in *Brown v. Board of Education* (1954) that segregated public schools were unconstitutional, leaders of the surging civil rights movement knew just where to go in the North to publicize their crusade. On February 2, 1959, Martin Luther King Jr. stood before the Liberty Bell to lay the customary wreath for the eighteenth observance of Freedom Day. Four years later, amid the furor over the Birmingham, Alabama, church bombing that took the lives of four black girls and King's "Letter from Birmingham Jail," the Philadelphia chapter of the Congress of Racial Equality (CORE) staged a sit-in at the Liberty Bell. The CORE members vowed to remain until President John Kennedy sent federal troops and voter registrars to Alabama.

The National Park Service now found itself in a delicate position. The *Philadelphia Inquirer* wagged its finger at those who would "give the appearance of trying to take over a historic shrine held in reverence and deep respect by responsible citizens, everywhere in the land." All-night sit-ins, it argued, "are more likely to harm than aid the cause they are intended to support."[33] Other local newspapers supported this position, and majority white public opinion held that if the protestors were not forcibly removed, other groups would follow their precedent for whatever cause they espoused. Civil rights activists countered that the day of depending on moral suasion to make the country live up to its founding principles was long over and that nonviolent confrontational tactics were morally justified.

Caught between these two arguments, the Park Service superintendent, Conrad L. Wirth, ordered that the sit-in protestors be allowed to remain overnight. The mayor of Philadelphia declared a day of mourning; throughout the city churches held special services. This persuaded the CORE sit-in protestors to withdraw from Independence Hall.[34]

Civil rights protest, 1965. Courtesy Independence
National Historical Park

The Liberty Bell, as some had warned, continued to be
a focal point for protests in the North as the civil rights
crisis intensified. In 1964 the Mississippi Freedom Summer Campaign had been countered by widespread white
violence in the South, including the kidnapping and murder of three young civil rights workers. Rock-ribbed seg-
regationists resisted school integration a decade after the
Supreme Court had ruled that it must proceed with
"deliberate speed." In 1965 the black Muslim activist
Malcolm X was assassinated by members of the Nation of

Islam; the Selma-to-Montgomery march across Pettus Bridge captured headlines; Congress passed the 1965 Voting Rights Act; and the worst urban upheaval in a century occurred in Watts, the south central area of Los Angeles.

By now it was nearly predictable that the sacred ground on which the Liberty Bell rested would be employed as the ideal place to rivet the public's attention on the civil rights crisis. After all, the inscription on the bell could not have been more relevant. Would full-throated liberty be proclaimed throughout the land and to all the inhabitants thereof? For African Americans, genuine freedom— social, legal, political, and economic—was still illusory.

For the National Park Service, charged with guarding the Liberty Bell and guiding visitors to see it, 1965 put the bell's inscription to the test. In February three men from the Black Liberation Front and one woman from the Quebec Separatist Movement planned to dynamite the Liberty Bell, the Washington Monument, and the Statue of Liberty. New York City police uncovered the abortive plot, and the terrorists were sentenced to long jail terms.[35] In March pickets and sit-in protestors, mostly students from Cheyney State College and the University of Pennsylvania, demonstrated to protest interference against voter registration drives in the South and the killing of a Boston clergyman working there. Despite

much public outcry, the Park Service decided not to in-
terfere with the sit-ins. "We are doing this," the superintendent announced, "because the Liberty Bell is a symbol for the people of the United States, and because we
do not believe American citizens should be forcibly removed from the Liberty Bell while they are giving peace-
ful expressions to their beliefs."[36] And so the year continued. The next year, the conservative Young Americans
for Freedom, arriving with the reigning Miss USA,
staged a rally at Independence Hall to counter civil rights
activists.

In the era of counterculture, the Liberty Bell proved as
irresistible to hippies and assorted free spirits as to political activists. In 1967 the bell was mobbed by a "be-in" of
several thousand young Americans, who shared distinc-
tively pungent cigarettes among themselves and showered arriving police cars with flowers and candy in a joy-
ful "un-birthday party."[37] In a more focused gathering,
the Liberty Bell looked down as the consumer activist
Ralph Nader presided over thousands of people at the
first Earth Day on April 22, 1970. Some conservative
groups, pointing out that this was the hundredth anniversary of Vladimir Lenin's birthday, tried to smear the
event as "a Communist trick." Nonetheless, twenty million Americans celebrated Earth Day nationwide, many
puzzled by the dark warning of a DAR representative that

"subversive elements plan to make American children live in an environment that is good for them."[38]

The Vietnam War also proved that the Liberty Bell was one of the nation's premier venues for protesting—or endorsing—government policy. Throughout the Cold War, the bell had been the symbol deployed recurrently in reaffirming the American and Western European struggle against Communism. But as early as April 1965, when President Lyndon Johnson muscled up American involvement in the war, one hundred college students staged an antiwar sit-in at Independence Hall. Young Americans for Freedom quickly staged a counterdemonstration, circling the bell to prevent its "desecration."[39] By 1969, with half a million Americans bogged down in a desperate war, with students protesting by hundreds of thousands at campuses across the country, and with the murdered Martin Luther King Jr. and Bobby Kennedy in their graves, war protestors repeatedly made their way to the Liberty Bell to try to change their nation's foreign policy.

To commemorate the death of the Communist leader Ho Chi Minh in Hanoi, a Haverford College professor of physics read excerpts from the North Vietnamese Declaration of Independence (fashioned by Ho in 1945 after the American Declaration of Independence). Chaos erupted. A hostile crowd of pro-war Philadelphians lunged to seize the rice bowl that the antiwar protestors had brought to place by the Liberty Bell alongside a bouquet of flowers. The *Philadelphia Inquirer* denounced the effort to honor Ho as "a disgusting scene" and "a form of [Liberty Bell] sacrilege if there ever was one." The pro-war supporters, disciples of Carl McIntire, a fundamentalist, right-wing preacher, returned three days later to conduct "a symbolic cleansing" of the Liberty Bell.[40] This much was now evident: in a democracy a price had to be paid for becoming the nation's most potent symbol of individual freedom. The liberty that the bell rang for was a liberty subject to many interpretations; and in the late twentieth century, its invocation of "Liberty throughout all the Land unto all the Inhabitants thereof" gave everyone a claim to the Liberty Bell.

The civil rights movement and the deeply divided public opinion on the Vietnam War both reached climaxes when the guardians of the Liberty Bell were preparing for the bicentennial of the Declaration of Independence. History was repeating itself, for one hundred years earlier much of the nation had been similarly roiled as the centennial celebration approached, albeit for different causes: industrial labor strikes and Indian wars on the Great Plains. In 1976, the nation did not concentrate its extravaganza in a single place, as in 1876, but celebrated the bicentennial everywhere in a true show of grassroots solidarity. Still, the mother of all celebrations was in Philadelphia, for that is where American scripture had been written.

The preparations for the bicentennial had been preceded by administrative changes that gave the Liberty Bell new custodians. Early in World War II, representatives of more than fifty patriotic and civic organizations had formed the Independence Hall Association, intent on wresting the supervision, maintenance, and enhancement of Independence Hall and its Liberty Bell from the City of Philadelphia. Only after the crowded, down-at-the-heels neighborhoods around Independence Hall were razed could these national treasures bask in their own glory and thus fully reveal to the public their historic significance.[41]

With this in mind, Pennsylvania appropriated funds at the end of World War II to buy three square blocks north of Independence Hall—a great jumble of warehouses, factories, office buildings, stores, and ramshackle, deteriorated dwellings—to create an "Independence Mall." Gradually, bulldozers demolished the area and added several feet of fill soil that sealed everything below the surface, including millions of fragments of the past—"buried history," as urban archaeologists call it—that later could be rescued from cisterns and privy shafts.

Of utmost importance was the agreement of the City of Philadelphia, after great controversy, to transfer custody of Independence Hall, including the Liberty Bell and a group of other historic structures, to the National Park Service. The title to the property would remain with the city, as it still does. But in 1948 Congress approved what would three years later become the Independence National Historical Park.[42] Now, park rangers in their smart outfits would lead tours of Independence Hall and the Liberty Bell.

This bold move brought federal dollars. Lots of them. Money for architectural, archaeological, and historical research, as well as the restoration of eighteenth-century buildings associated with the American Revolution that the Park Service began to acquire, has poured from Washington ever since. This has permitted the meticulous restoration of many historic structures—such as the Dolley Todd Madison House, the First and Second Banks of the United States, Carpenters' Hall, and Military Hall, where the U.S. Marine Corps was born. Millions of dollars have gone into programs for engaging the public's interest in the history of Independence Hall, the Liberty Bell, and associated revolutionary-era buildings. Penn's City of Brotherly Love had lovingly cared for its sick patient, its crack widening noticeably over many decades and its surface worn by the touches, kisses, and tappings of thousands of people, both in the city and on the road. Now the National Park Service shouldered the responsibilities. But the Park Service would soon learn that Philadelphians insisted on their claim—social and political, if not legal—to the Liberty Bell's location and the manner of its display.

Almost from the beginning of its custodianship of the Liberty Bell, the Park Service wanted to remove it from Independence Hall in order to protect and interpret it more effectively on ground of its own. But public opposition in 1958 stalled this effort. While biding its time, the Park Service gave the Liberty Bell a new persona. Edward R. Murrow, the famed CBS radio newscaster whose reports from Europe during World War II had made him a household name, became the voice of the bell. In a recorded four-minute talk, brought to life at the push of a button, Murrow explained the history and symbolism of the treasured bell. "Mute Liberty Bell Speaks and the Voice is Murrow's," boasted the *Evening Bulletin.* "This bell," the visitor heard, "has played a greater role in history than any other bell in the world. Cracked and mute, resting silently here in the corridor of Independence Hall, it has been heard in the hearts of freedom-loving people throughout the world." Murrow recounted the hoary tale that the bell had cracked on July 8, 1835, while tolling the death of John Marshall, chief justice of the Supreme Court, conceding that this was "how tradition has it" rather than established fact.[43]

In 1968, with the national bicentennial approaching, the National Park Service renewed its effort to find a new location for the Liberty Bell. Anticipating some forty million visitors—this turned out to be a grossly exaggerated estimate—the service argued that Independence Hall would be swamped during the six-month celebration, producing a crowd-control nightmare. If the bell remained at the bottom of the vestibule, where the stairway led to the second floor, the massed visitors, quipped a Park Service assistant superintendent, would be "forced to faint vertically instead of horizontally." Opposition to any relocation was intense, much of it from city and state officials. But the Park Service finally prevailed after three years of controversy.[44]

At first the plan was to move the Liberty Bell three blocks to a new tower to be erected as part of a Visitors Center at Third and Chestnut streets. That plan gave way to a new glass-walled pavilion, later to be derided as an architectural failure, a moment's walk from Independence Hall. Opening ceremonies at 12:01 A.M. on January 1, 1976, ushering in the bicentennial, drew a large crowd, much pageantry, and a chilling rain.[45] For the next twenty-seven years, the pavilion would be the Liberty Bell's new home.

Plans for the bicentennial provided moments of mirth about the venerable American icon. The Whitechapel Bell Foundry, which cast the first State House Bell in 1752

Liberty Bell in the Bicentennial Pavilion, 1995. Park Service rangers still allowed visitors to touch, kiss, and caress the bell. Courtesy Independence National Historical Park

and has remained in business since 1570, offered to make 2,400 twenty-pound replicas of the Liberty Bell and turn over the first bell to "a pretty Philadelphia school teacher in a long white gown with red and blue trim" who would bring the bell back to Philadel-phia as a gift. Each of the others would be sold at $756—clapper, bell cord, and supporting oak plaque included—to patriotic groups, historical societies, and private collectors. The bell would not have a crack because, as the Whitechapel officers slyly implied, the original bell had left London undamaged.[46]

Some Philadelphians, maintaining levity, saw this simply as a profit-making venture sponsored by a phantom Liberty Bell Foundation in London, which indeed turned out to have been formed by a former journalist, an oil company director, and a canny public relations man. Forming the "Procrastinators' Club of America," forty Philadelphians, carrying signs reading "We got a lemon," vowed to picket the Whitechapel Bell Foundry in London and demand a new, crackless bell. "We want it to look good for the Bicentennial," explained the club's president. "After all, it's embarrassing for the most affluent nation in the world to have a busted bell as the symbol of its freedom."

Whitechapel's co-owner played along. He apologized that Thomas Lester, who had cast the original bell 218 years before, would not be able to greet the Procrastinators' Club delegates "as he has been in a permanent state of procrastination since 1776." As for providing a replacement bell, Whitechapel recounted the judgment made in 1752 that the bell had been cast properly, its cracking the result of colonial carelessness. But to be generous, as the United States approached the bicentennial of the Declaration of Independence, the foundry offered to recast the bell if the cracked one was returned "in its original carton." That ended the badinage.[47]

It was a busy year for the Whitechapel Foundry. On commission, it cast a twelve thousand–pound bell (six times as large as the original bell), which was hung in the new National Park Service Visitor Center, where it remains today. Queen Elizabeth II presented the bell on July 16, 1976, and read its inscription: "For the people of the United States from the people of Britain, 4 July 1976, Let Freedom Ring." The entrepreneur Edward Piszek, president of Mrs. Paul's Kitchen, a frozen fish company, commissioned another replica of the Liberty Bell. He soon purchased a two-centuries-old house at Third and Pine streets, where the patriot Tadeuz Kościuszko had lived briefly in 1797–98, and donated it to Independence National Historical Park to become part of its complex of revolutionary-era sites.[48] The mayor of Jerusalem spearheaded the commissioning of a replica Liberty Bell and helped raise money from schoolchildren. Installed in Liberty Bell Park, the bell stands quietly in his city's most popular park.

Throughout the bicentennial, the Liberty Bell was a featured icon. The U.S. Mint produced a half-dollar coin with the Liberty Bell on one side and a dollar coin with the bell backgrounded by a full moon. The newly independent U.S. Postal Service added to the catalogue of Liberty Bell stamps—the 1926 issue had been joined by airmail stamps in 1960 and 1961—with a thirteen-cent stamp in 1975 for the Bicentennial. (Other stamps with the Liberty Bell image would follow, including a 2007 issue.) Appearing on millions of envelopes, the Liberty Bell stamps have kept the treasured icon before the public's eye for years.

The bicentennial marked the beginning of a new era for the Liberty Bell. With the bell ensconced in its own glass-and-brick pavilion, its story could be told by park rangers apart from Independence Hall. Independence Hall's story was mainly an eighteenth-century affair, while the Liberty Bell's importance had gained momentum in the nineteenth and twentieth centuries. This difference was magnified by the Park Service's decision that, while the ground around Independence Hall should be reserved for patriotic celebrations, the new pavilion for the Liberty Bell was space that "encourages the guaranteed exercise of free speech and assembly."[49] Various groups have taken full advantage of this provision, especially on the Fourth of July. Every year since 1986, for example, the Martin Luther King Association for Non-Violence holds a ceremony at the bell on the commemoration of King's birthday. In 1992 several hundred abortion-rights demonstrators occupied the Liberty Bell pavilion chanting, "No choice, no liberty." Three years later, a group supporting the homeless camped overnight in the shadow of the pavilion to dramatize the need for affordable housing.

In 1999 supporters of Mumia Abu-Jamal, a death-row inmate in a Pennsylvania prison, took over the pavilion for several hours.[50]

Standing apart from Independence Hall, the Liberty Bell pavilion became a magnet of great force. Rather than waiting in line to be guided through Independence Hall by park rangers, people often bypassed the venerable building to visit the Liberty Bell, where they could file through the pavilion more readily, gaze at the Old Bell, bearing the scars of history with dignity, and touch it. Throughout the 1980s an average of about 1.5 million each year visited the Liberty Bell, and in the 1990s that number held steady, in every year about twice the number who visited Independence Hall.[51]

After the terrorist attacks of September 11, 2001, Washington directed the Independence National Historical Park to impose security measures that greatly restricted the flow of visitors to both Independence Hall and the Liberty Bell Pavilion. In recent years, these restrictions, which included electronic checking of handbags and barriers to control the flow of visitors, have been eased. But the Park Service still struggles as the allocation of funds diverted to security measures starves other parts of its operations.

FIVE

Everyone's Liberty Bell

Picking up the *New York Times, Washington Post, Philadelphia Inquirer, Wall Street Journal, Dallas Morning News,* or *USA Today* on April 1, 1996, readers nearly spilled their coffee when reading that the restaurant chain Taco Bell had purchased the Liberty Bell. In a full-page ad, the fast-food giant announced that it had made the purchase for an undisclosed amount "in an effort to help the national debt." Furthermore, it disclosed that "one of our country's most historic treasures . . . will now be called the 'Taco Liberty Bell.'" A separate press release added details: the Taco Liberty Bell would split its time between Philadelphia and the Taco Bell headquarters in Irvine, California. The company hoped other corporations would similarly "do their part to reduce the country's debt."

Citizens flooded the Independence National Historical Park's phone lines to express their shock that the Liberty Bell had been sold and to vent their anger over the company's boast that "Taco Bell's heritage and imagery have revolved around the symbolism of the [Liberty] bell. Now we've got the crown jewel of bells."

Rushing into action, the Park Service called a press conference to deny they had sold the Liberty Bell. In fact, it still belonged to the City of Philadelphia. Within hours, Taco Bell issued a press release confessing that the ad was a hoax. After all, it was issued on April Fool's Day. Sniffing great profits from all the publicity it had gained, the company proposed to donate fifty thousand dollars for the upkeep of the bell.

The Clinton White House, seeing some humor in the situation, directed its press secretary to tell reporters that on behalf of its privatization efforts they had arranged for the Ford Motor Company to refurbish the Lincoln Memorial. Hereafter, it would be called the Lincoln Mercury Memorial.

Many found the Taco Bell hoax distasteful, if not sacrilegious. One op-ed writer in the *Washington Times* called it a "cheap, thoughtless advertising ploy [that is] totally disgusting. To use this sacred symbol as part of some silly game is an affront to generations of proud Americans who have fought and died for this country's freedom—so proudly represented by the Liberty Bell." But the Liberty Bell had been commodified for years in a hundred different ways. Which in fact testified to its secure place as an American icon. Taco Bell publicists played it both ways. They had garnered millions of dollars of free publicity from the seventy million Americans exposed to the hoax in newspaper, radio, and television coverage, including *The Today Show*, NBC's *Nightly News*, and the *Wall Street Journal*'s radio program *This Morning*. Sales of burritos, tacos, and enchiladas rose by a half-million dollars in the week of the ad. But at the same time, Taco Bell executives claimed, the hoax gave a tremendous amount of recognition to the Liberty Bell and the need to maintain it properly.[1]

There comes a point when an icon is so deeply etched in the public mind that anyone with an ounce of capitalistic energy and a nose for low-hanging fruit will jump to seek profit. In Philadelphia, the Liberty Bell's home, one can't go very far without encountering the commercial use of the bell. At the National League Phillies' baseball stadium (now Citizens Bank Park!), a gigantic Liberty Bell above the right field bleachers lights up and rings whenever a Phillie hits a home run. On the other side of town, the ponies ran at the Liberty Bell Racetrack from 1963 to 1986 (until it was demolished to make way for Walmart and other big-box outlets). Up the Schuylkill River at Douglasville, the Liberty Bell Motorsports Park and Campground caters to Harley-Davidson bikers, while across the Delaware River from Philadelphia at Mount Laurel, sailors go for blue ribbons at the Liberty Bell Regatta.

All around the city—and elsewhere—for-profit outfits eagerly capitalize on the Liberty Bell. Hang out at the Liberty Belle nightclub near the Philadelphia Navy Yard. Or buy insurance from the Liberty Bell Life Insurance Company. Or deposit your paycheck with Liberty Bell Bank; get title insurance for your home from the Liberty Bell Agency; make your car's engine hum with Liberty Bell Oil; sign up (if you live in the Denver area) with Liberty Bell Telecom; mount up and ride to the sound of guns on a saddle from Liberty Bell Tack Shop; dress up your living room with new Liberty Bell Windows; get ready for the Labor Day barbeque with top sirloin from Liberty Bell Steak Company; do a backyard makeover with walls and fountains from Liberty Bell Precast Stone Company; call in Liberty Bell Catering for your next party; or protect your house by calling the Liberty Bell Alarm Company. If you are lonely in Bear Creek, Montana, Liberty Belle will be your escort to whatever venue strikes your fancy.

Anything else needed? For your pet parrot, what about a nickel-plated Liberty Bell to dangle in the cage? A

"Liberty Bell Patriotic Handcrafted Cat and Dog Pillow Pad"? A Nestlé chocolate Liberty Bell ("shelf life of one year if properly stored at room temperature")? A Liberty Bell luggage lock? A "Liberty Bell March" ringtone? A Liberty Bell T-shirt announcing, "I Came to Philly for the Crack" ($18.95, choice of eleven colors)? The "Liberty Bell Classic Thong" from several undergarment manufacturers (the bell's image in front, the only space available)? For the sexually adventurous, the "Liberty Bell Couples Toy" (available online or at most sex shops for about forty dollars)? A little less exotic are Liberty Bell nipple and navel rings. Or—for specialists only—a Liberty Bell patch from the California Gang Investigators Association promises untold rewards.

Turning the Liberty Bell into something marketable is one thing; using it to pull on people's patriotism to sell an unrelated product is another. Almost as soon as advertising became big business in the late nineteenth century, agencies seized on the Liberty Bell to push the products of their clients. Corporations with war-production contracts took naturally to this trend. Anaconda Copper, Doak Aircraft Company, and Western World Champion Ammunition, among others, splattered the Liberty Bell on their ads. But other products as varied as Chase and Sanborn coffee, Anheuser-Busch's Budweiser beer, Campbell's soup, Waukesha ginger ale, and Prince Albert tobacco tried to loosen pocketbooks with flashy ads featuring the Liberty Bell. The colonial revival that swept suburban home architecture in the post–World War II period pumped up the output of home furnishing items by replicating the bell. Now a patriotic American could have a Liberty Bell showerhead, a Liberty Bell teapot (with the crack sealed), or an AM radio with a miniature Liberty Bell mounted on it. More recently, you can buy a decorative plate with Snoopy sleeping happily on his back atop the Liberty Bell, a Liberty Bell slot machine, and a Kentucky bourbon whiskey bottle shaped like the Liberty Bell. The journey from revered historic relic to emblem of consumer capitalism seems to be complete.

As the Liberty Bell's fame grew, poets, musicians, and artists cashed in. This in turn furthered the business of making the Liberty Bell a household word and almost *the* American icon. But as we will see, the way poetry, art, and music have popularized the Liberty Bell has changed— and not always in the tradition of tethering it to patriotism.

Poems about the Liberty Bell go back to the 1840s, when it was adopted as the abolitionists' symbol, as we have seen. Children's magazines, such as *Youth's Companion*, were publishing poems about the noble bell by the late nineteenth century, one poignantly calling the jagged crack in the bell as "sacred as the battle-wound of which a conqueror died."[2] At the 1876 Philadelphia Centennial

COPPER...

Helps freedom ring

It was the ringing voice of copper that on July 4th, 1776, proclaimed "LIBERTY THROUGH-OUT ALL THE LAND UNTO ALL THE INHABITANTS THEREOF." Today, copper, in the form of gleaming strands of wire, carries to the world the news which helps to keep men free.

Were it not for copper, modern communication systems would be practically non-existent. For telephone and telegraph, radio and television can speed our word or image to its farthest destination as swiftly as light itself; but only because copper provides a pathway for the electricity that gives life to these communications.

More than the "voice" of freedom, copper is its strong helping hand, too. For copper, and its alloys brass and bronze, play a vital role in enabling free men to make in abundance the products that keep our economy strong.

Anaconda, foremost in copper, brass and bronze, is proud that the products of its mines and mills are helping to strengthen the cause of Freedom.

ANACONDA

First in Copper, Brass and Bronze

"Anaconda" is a registered trademark.   91232

Forty-nine exact replicas of the famous Liberty Bell have been presented by the Copper Industry to the Treasury Department. It was Copper, the Voice of Liberty, that on May 15th announced the opening of the 1950 Independence Savings Bond Drive.

Advertisement for Anaconda Copper featuring the Liberty Bell, 1950. As of May 2009, the Google online search engine yielded more than 1.4 million "hits" for the Liberty Bell; a large fraction of them pertain to the use of the Liberty Bell for commercial purposes.

Exposition sheet music of "The Liberty Bell" made tidy profits for its composer. The bell's road trips from 1885 to 1915 invariably got poets and musicians busy on Liberty Bell derivatives. For the departure of the bell on its way west to the Chicago World's Fair in 1893, the Philadelphia Symphony, under the baton of Ignacy Jan Paderewski, played a farewell concert. That inspired a distinctly amateur poet to compose a witty poem titled "The Liberty Bell Parade":

> I did not hear the Paderooskey
> Playing so dexterously, each loose key
> Rippling 'neath his facile hands,
> The tones, from many foreign lands,
> Of great composers; true, I missed
> The rhapsodies of Wagner, Liszt,
> Beethoven, Chopin—all the throng
> That gave the world its best of song;
> Playing in *forte* and in *douce* key,
> I did not hear Paderooskey
>
> But when the noisy populace
> Surged in the crowded public place
> To see the "Bell Procession" go
> I heard a martial music throw
> Its spell in glad, undying songs

That nerved our Fathers, fighting wrongs,
Across the multitudes that swayed
Beneath the blaring bands that played
Songs hushed upon the Prospect Newsky,
And never played by Paderewski

And made rough men and women feel
The sacredness of common weal.
Lo, as they listened, came the Bell
Of Liberty, whose tocsin knell
Startled a king-rule Isle and made
The tyrant on his throne afraid.
Oh, better the "Red, White and Blue's" Key
Than all things played by Paderooskey.[3]

Once in Chicago, the Liberty Bell attracted the attention of John Philip Sousa, whose "Liberty Bell March," first played by his eighty-six-piece band, was a huge hit. "The Song of the Liberty Bell" (1904), "The Liberty Bell March and Two Step" (1906), "Emblem of Liberty March" (1907), and "You're a Grand Old Bell" (1909) kept Americans musically in touch with the bell. Even a patriotic, romantic operatic attempt, *The Liberty Bell*, was tried on Philadelphians in 1898 (with scant success).[4]

Then came World War I. Even before the United States entered the war, sales of "The Song of the Liberty Bell,"

"Liberty Bell Waltz," and "Bell of Bells" sold briskly as sheet music. But the big hit, "Liberty Bell (It's Time to Ring Again)," came in 1917:

> You have rest-ed, Lib-er-ty Bell, for a hun-dred
>   years and more,
> End your slum-ber Lib-er-ty Bell, ring as you did
>   be-fore,
> It's time to wake 'em up, it's time to shake 'em up,
> It's a cause worth ring-ing for:
>
> Lib-er-ty Bell, it's time to ring a-gain,
> Lib-er-ty Bell, it's time to swing a-gain,
> We're in the same sort of fix, we were in sev-en-ty-six,
> And we are read-y to mix and ral-ly 'round you like
>   we did be-fore, oh!
> Lib-er-ty Bell, your voice is need-ed now,
> Lib-er-ty Bell, we'll hear your call, one and all,
> Though you're old and there's a crack in you
> Don't for-get Old Glor-y's back-in' you,
> Oh! Lib-er-ty Bell, it's time to ring a-gain.

After the war, composers couldn't stop trying to make the Hit Parade with Liberty Bell songs. Among them were "My Own Liberty Bell," published for the Philadelphia Sesquicentennial Exposition in 1926; "Congratulations Liberty Bell," played as Franklin D. Roosevelt entered the White House; "Bells of Freedom," recorded in 1938; and then, at the end of World War II, "The Song of Our Liberty Bell." All of these renditions were melodious, patriotic, and fuzzy warm.

Songsters were never at a loss in trying to keep the Liberty Bell in everyone's mind. But they changed their tune once the nation reached the mid-twentieth century. By this time the day was long past since a large majority of Americans had seen and touched the Liberty Bell as it toured the country again and again. And no longer did most children read heartwarming poems and stories about the Liberty Bell or sing Henry Clay Work's "Ring the Bell." For them, the Liberty Bell no longer figured in their bedtime prayers.

As the age of counterculture swept the nation in the 1960s, the Liberty Bell still rang, but much differently. To be sure, Sousa's "Liberty Bell March" continued to be played—by the U.S. Air Force Band of the Rockies on its "Hands Across the Sea" album, by the U.S. Marine Corps Band at both the Bill Clinton and George W. Bush presidential inaugurals; and, though most viewers probably didn't know it, as background music as the opening titles flew by for the wildly popular *Monty Python's Flying Circus* television shows from 1969 to 1973. However, most of the music co-opting the Liberty Bell in recent decades has not been exactly patriotic. From the Lightning Guitar of Jimmy Bryant came the lively "Liberty Bell Polka" (2003), but much else has been downright raucous. The heavyweight champion and sometimes singer Muhammad Ali's "Who Knocked the Crack in the Liberty Bell?" (the answer is "Ali, Ali") was a highlight of *Ali and His Gang vs. Mr. Tooth Decay.* "Liberty Bell and the Black Diamond Express" by the Go-Betweens, an alternative and punk rock group, is strictly for nonconformist youth. The 2006 hip-hop recording "Liberty Bell" is by DJ Clue? featuring Beanie Sigel, Cassidy, and Freeway; and the heavy metal group If Hope Dies's "Let Freedom Ring from the Taco Liberty Bell" (2004) is unabashedly alternative with lines like

Smash apart the stones
Piled high upon our chests
And take in our first
Breaths of freedom.

Naturally, the oceans are no barrier. Nathania, a Thai power metal group, amps up to pound out "Liberty Bell Rang" (2004).

Moviemakers have given the Liberty Bell (or Liberty Belle) a split personality. Juliette Binoche's first big-screen role was in *Liberty Belle* (1983), a film set in post–World War II Paris, where students enlist in a movement to oppose the French suppression of the Algerian liberation movement. Here, the Liberty Bell was symbolically enlisted in a war for self-determination, but Hollywood could cast the bell very differently in a horror flick. In *Blow Out* (1981), Brian De Palma casts John Lithgow as a renegade secret service agent turned slasher hitman; his character carves holes in the shape of the Liberty Bell in the abdomens of his prostitute victims—and thus becomes known as the Liberty Bell Stalker. John Travolta plays a sound technician in Philadelphia who works on soft-core porn films. At the end of the movie viewers see a monster parade, with floats, marching bands, and a huge balloon in the shape of the Liberty Bell proceeding through downtown Philadelphia to celebrate Liberty Day.

Some sobersided media producers returned the Liberty Bell to respectability or at least harmless fun. Such was the case with "Liberty Bell," the theme song of the PBS American Revolution series titled *Liberty!* (1997), whose haunting background music features James Taylor singing "Johnny's Gone for a Soldier" and Yo-Yo Ma and Wynton Marsalis providing instrumentals. Meanwhile, on the popular situation comedy *How I Met Your Mother*, Barney is kinky but lovable as he indulges his desire to lick things. Among his favorites are national monuments such as the Washington Monument, the Golden Gate Bridge, the Alamo, and—of course—the Liberty Bell. A giant of the communications world, Stuart Prebble, CEO of ITV Digital, in 2002 set up Liberty Bell Productions, which now handles some of Great Britain's leading comedians and television shows, thus bringing the Liberty Bell to the attention of millions even if its artists don't traffic in the bell itself.

The trend in the plastic arts has paralleled changes in musical appropriations of the Liberty Bell. In the days of our grandparents, the illustrator N. C. Wyeth's *Ringing Out Liberty* (1930) was the first of the patriotic posters commissioned by the Pennsylvania Railroad. During the Great Depression, the J. C. Leyendecker *Saturday Evening Post* cover for July 6, 1935, has George Lippard's old bell ringer gonging the Liberty Bell. Leyendecker's successor as cover artist for the *Post*, Norman Rockwell, did a traditional July Fourth magazine cover and then, in one of his last works, painted himself in 1976 draping a "Happy Birthday" banner on the Liberty Bell in observance of the two hundredth anniversary of the Declaration of Independence.

In today's anything-goes world, artists have eroticized the Liberty Bell. Jeff Koons, who grew up in York, Pennsylvania, west of Philadelphia, includes an image of the Liberty Bell in an erotic assemblage for his "Hulk Elvis" series. Formerly married to Ilona Staller, the Hungarian-Italian porn star who later won election to the Italian Parliament, Koons professes that politics were not in his mind in including the Liberty Bell. But he is not the only artist who has made the Liberty Bell, or the Liberty Belle, into titillating or pornographic art.

Comic books—art in a different form—have made up in part for the disappearance of the Liberty Bell poems and songs in the schools. In DC Comics, Jesse Chambers, later to adopt her mother's name, Liberty Belle, is the daughter of Johnny Quick. Liberty Belle inherits her parents' supernatural power in fighting her way through World War II and, during the Cold War, in trying to defuse a nuclear threat. In her tight-fitting outfit with a Liberty Bell decorating her chest, the younger Liberty Belle became a favorite for young Americans of the past several decades.

Also beamed at American youth is the full-sized replica of Independence Hall with the Liberty Bell ("authentically" cracked) at the Knott's Berry Farm amusement park in southern California; the exhibit opened on July 6, 1976. At nearby Disneyland, kids flock to Liberty Square and clamber aboard the riverboat *Liberty Bell* for a ten-minute cruise around a make-believe waterway.

Nearly everything that walks and makes sounds has gone forth in life under the Liberty Bell (or Belle) moniker, including dogs, cats, rabbits, horses, mules, donkeys, mice, parrots, canaries, and assorted songbirds. Yachts, sailboats, cruise ships, and race cars are proudly named the *Liberty Bell(e)*. Streets, lanes, circles, and cul-de-sacs are named Liberty Bell in Calabasas, California; Weymouth, Massachusetts; San Antonio, Texas; and Libertyville, Illinois. A flea market in Indianapolis; a Rastafarian temple in Silver Lake, California; a pawn shop in Bell, Florida; a restaurant in South Boston and another in Woburn, Massachusetts; a village in New Jersey—all are named Liberty Bell. Naturally, babies, especially if the parents' surname is Bell, are named Liberty without gender distinction.

All of this makes clear that the Liberty Bell has long permeated every aspect of American life. Popular culture has embraced the Liberty Bell. Scores of American entrepreneurs have linked their companies' names and advertising campaigns to the patriotism engendered by the Liberty Bell. Adulation of the bell for its universal message has swept the globe. And federal and state governments have placed the Liberty Bell in the service of their own political and diplomatic agendas. By the sunset of the twentieth century, the table had been set for Independence National Historical Park to create a new platform for the Liberty Bell that would carry it into the next century.

Planning for a new Liberty Bell home began in the early 1990s. The chosen site was at Sixth and Market streets, right across from a new Independence Visitor Center and only a block from Independence Hall. Private funders promised thirteen million dollars, and the new pavilion would have ample space to introduce the public to the Liberty Bell's venerable history and its many meanings at home and abroad over the past two centuries.

Here was a rare opportunity. Since 1976 the cracked bell had stood unadorned in a pavilion with limited space for any kind of interpretation that would help visitors to refresh their memories of what many nostalgically think of as the golden age, when the Liberty Bell first came to Philadelphia in the mid-eighteenth century.

Now was the chance to lead visitors forward through a long, wide passage toward the bell, which would stand in front of a plate-glass south-facing wall with a line of sight directly to Independence Hall. But what should occupy that space? Might the curators and exhibit designers find ways to contextualize the Liberty Bell, to pique public curiosity about its many lives, to raise questions about how its meaning had been contested, adapted, and adopted over more than two hundred years?

Equally challenging—and problem-strewn—was the matter of how INHP should treat the Liberty Bell's new site. The plot at Sixth and Market streets was not simply another piece of Philadelphia real estate; it happened to be one of the most history-soaked pieces of urban ground to be found on the East Coast of North America. This is where the widow of William Masters—mighty merchant, Philadelphia mayor in the 1750s, and the city's largest slaveowner—had erected a fine structure in 1767–68. In 1772, after William died, his widow gave the mansion to her daughter Polly when she married slaveowning Richard Penn, grandson of William Penn, Pennsylvania's founder. The house's next occupant, shortly after the Revolution erupted, was Sir William Howe, the British general leading the army that occupied Philadelphia from September 1777 to June 1778. After the British decamped, Benedict Arnold arrived to declare martial law and occupy the Masters-Penn mansion, with two enslaved Africans among his household retinue of seven. Then in 1781, Robert Morris, who has been called the financier of the American Revolution, purchased the house and began to reconstruct it, partly with the labor of his several slaves. Thus, for the entire revolutionary period, the lives of the free and unfree mingled intimately on this piece of Philadelphia soil.[5]

The presence of slaves on the site continued when Morris leased the house to George Washington for his executive mansion after the nation's capital moved from New York to Philadelphia in 1790. The new nation's first president made alterations, especially for sheltering a household staff of about thirty—a mixed lot of white indentured servants, hired hands, and nine enslaved African Americans from Mount Vernon. Thus each day after the new Liberty Bell Center opened, thousands of visitors would walk directly over the threshold of the first president's executive quarters, where freedom and slavery were entwined.

Both issues—how to present a rich interpretation of the many lives of America's premier historic relic and whether to use the thirteen thousand square feet of space outside the Liberty Bell pavilion, where thousands of visitors would line up while waiting to see the treasured icon—presented INHP with a rare opportunity to provide one of the nation's most important informal history classrooms. Site and symbol, freedom and slavery, black and white, upstairs and downstairs: how should the National Park Service explain the Liberty Bell and the site it would now occupy to the visitors who would swarm every year to venerate the bell?

The National Park Service was already committed to addressing previously neglected and controversial topics, including the history of slavery and Native American history.[6] In a step emblematic of its leaders' broader vision, the Park Service had signed a cooperative agreement in 1995 with the Organization of American Historians whereby individual sites could draw on professional historians to deepen their planned interpretations. Then in late 1999 the Northeast Region of NPS, to which INHP reports, became a founding member of the International Coalition of Historic Sites of Conscience. The undertaking of this coalition was much the same—to produce new exhibits and to train rangers and seasonal guides at historic sites in ways that would look history in the face and blend commemoration with critique. To this end, the NPS Northeast Region director, Marie Rust, launched the Civic Engagement Initiative, which put out a straightforward message: "In a democratic society such as ours, it is important to understand the journey of liberty and justice, together with the economic, social, religious, and other forces that barred or opened the ways for our ancestors, and the distances yet to be covered."[7]

That was the picture at the national and regional levels. But at the local level, where superintendents have much autonomy to protect their turf, the initiative was not embraced. Collaborative interpretative planning for the new Liberty Bell Center with scholars and the public was largely ignored, and the INHP superintendent decided to remain silent about the new site, where the president's house once stood. The reasons are probably best explained by a former INHP staffer, Jill Ogline, who believes that "creating dissonance for visitors" was "the park's greatest fear." This dissonance was exactly what the INHP superintendent believed would result from introducing freedom's complex and symbiotic embrace of slavery at the Liberty Bell site, both inside and outside the pavilion. "Not only acknowledging the Liberty Bell's proximity to a site upon which enslaved people toiled, but actually integrating that story of enslavement into the bell's narrative of freedom," Ogline believes, "might possibly be the greatest dissonance ever to be interpreted at a national historic site." Yet dissonance is not synonymous with dissatisfaction, alienation, or anger; and nuanced feeling and contemplation are often the product of dissonance. At the national and regional levels, "an intellectually unsettled visitor" was what the Park Service civic engagement proponents hoped for. After all, would not this be a sign of a citizen in a mature democracy who would not hate the Park Service but thank its rangers for telling hidden stories, uncovering buried ironies and paradoxes, and provoking thought?[8]

It distressed INHP's leaders that their several years of planning the Liberty Bell exhibit—which involved blocking out a number of zones of interpretation, selecting images, and writing captions and introductory paragraphs on the wall—erupted in sharp, even venomous debate. In early 2002, I was part of a group of historians and institutional leaders in Philadelphia, organized as the Ad Hoc Historians, who sharply criticized the interpretive plan that had already been put in the hands of the exhibit designers. Through radio and television interviews and press coverage, the group stirred enough interest to get the issue onto the front page of the *Philadelphia Inquirer*, onto its op-ed pages, and into Associated Press wire stories.

Our concern was twofold: that the exhibits planned for the new venue, though rich with material on the bell's history, would slight the fact that the Liberty Bell had been as much an inspiration to those still struggling for freedom as a celebration of freedom already achieved; and that the historical significance of the site of the new pavilion would be ignored almost entirely, noted only on a "wayside panel" out on the Market Street curb. In a radio interview with Marty Moss-Coane, hostess of WHYY's *Radio Times*, I blurted out that "our memory of the past is often managed and manipulated; here it is being downright buried." The switchboard began to light up as people called in from all compass points. Overwhelmingly, they supported my plea for presenting the history of the Liberty Bell site, along with the bell, in ways that mingled stories of freedom and unfreedom, black and white, mighty and humble, leaving the public with food for thought rather than simply a warm, cozy glow about the old cracked bell.

Fifteen minutes of discussion about the Liberty Bell on *Radio News* proved a crucial turning point. The public was getting aroused. Equally important, Stephan Salisbury at the *Philadelphia Inquirer* decided to cover the story. Writing with the architectural critic Inga Saffron, he splashed the story on the Sunday front page, March 24, 2003, with a headline reading "Echoes of Slavery at Liberty Bell Site." Thousands of *Inquirer* readers now learned about a chapter of forgotten history—"the presence of slaves at the heart of one of the nation's most potent symbols of freedom." Salisbury and Saffron included a defensive statement from the Park Service that "the Liberty Bell is its own story, and Washington's slaves are a different one better told elsewhere." They quoted Philadelphia's African-American mayor, John Street, as being disturbed by the curtailment of history and calling for "a very earnest dialogue . . . about how to address the issue of Washington and his slaves." Randall Miller, the former editor of the *Pennsylvania Magazine of History and Biography* and a prolific author from St. Joseph's University, was quoted at length, pointing out that Park Service was missing an opportunity "to tell the real story of the American Revolution and the meaning of freedom. Americans, through Washington, were working out the definition of freedom in a new republic. And Washington had slaves. Meanwhile, the slaves were defining freedom for themselves by running away. There are endless contradictions embedded in this site."[9]

Two days later, the *Inquirer* devoted a full page to the

issue, with a clever headline "Site Unseen" about the Morris-Washington house, along with an article about Mayor Street's dialogue with Park Service officials, who now seemed willing to rethink their exhibits, especially if the mayor agreed that work on the new pavilion would not be delayed. Meanwhile, Miller and I worked with the Ad Hoc Historians, which included the directors of most of Philadelphia's history-related institutions, to hold the feet of Park Service officials to the fire while offering to work with them to rethink their plans for the Liberty Bell Center and the site on which it would rise.

Turning up the heat, the *Inquirer's* March 27 lead editorial was headlined "Freedom and Slavery: Just as They Coexisted in the 1700s, Both Must Be Part of Liberty Bell's Story." The *Inquirer* wagged its finger at the Park Service administrators, reminding them that "the old cracked bell will be situated on ground that enhances it as a cherished symbol of the struggle for liberty, especially to African Americans." The editorial expressed confidence that "the Liberty Bell in its new home will not bury an ugly part of the country's history."

Meanwhile, Randall Miller and I drafted an op-ed piece for the *Inquirer.* We were mindful that for several years, the city's most widely read newspaper had rejected various op-ed pieces written by Edward Lawler on "A Forgotten Landmark," in which he explained how many wonderful stories could enlighten, entertain, and challenge mythical remembrances of the past if only INHP would broaden its vision. Why not, Lawler asked, restore the public's memory of the Morris mansion? Why not talk about the young John Quincy Adams sitting in the front hall with President Washington and seventeen visiting Chickasaw chiefs, passing an enormous ceremonial peace pipe around the circle? Or Nelly Custis and her grandmother, the first lady, preparing for bed and kneeling in prayer before Nelly sang Martha to sleep. Or a frank discussion of Washington's slaveholding at the mansion, including his pursuit of those who took flight. "Rather than shrinking from this historical fact," Lawler had written, "INHP should embrace the challenge that it presents and use it to give visitors a more complex and complete view of American history," to "make it tangible that slavery was not an institution confined to the South" and to invite visitors to consider that the history of slavery and the history of the Liberty Bell were "inextricably entwined."

In our op-ed essay, Miller and I argued that the Park Service should enlist historians to help bring out the rich stories showing "that freedom and slavery commingled at the Liberty Bell site and elsewhere." "Washington was the living symbol of freedom and independence," we wrote, and "Washington's slaves were living symbols of the most paradoxical part of the nation's birth—freedom and unfreedom side by side, with the enslavement of some making possible the liberty of others. An exhibition of documents and artifacts should show slavery's and freedom's many meanings at the dawn of the new nation. Doing so will make the Liberty Bell's own story ring loud and true." We concluded: "A free people dare not bury evidence or silence long-forgotten African Americans, whose stories make the meaning of the Liberty Bell and the Revolution real and palpable, here and abroad." The essay appeared on Easter Sunday, March 31, along with one by Charlene Mires, a historian at Villanova University whose book on Independence Hall was soon to be published. An eye-catching image dominated the op-ed page: a slave's ankle shackles superimposed on a replica of the Declaration of Independence. The next day, the Associated Press put a story on the wire, to be picked up around the country, titled "Historians Decry Liberty Bell Site." The entwined history of freedom and slavery on Independence Mall was now becoming a hot issue.

Moving from publicity to concrete results hinged on getting the Park Service to work with our growing committee. The intervention of the National Park Service's chief historian, Dwight Pitcaithley, became crucially important in this effort. When he first saw the interpretative plan, Pitcaithley was shocked to find a chest-thumping, celebratory script, "an exhibit to make people feel good but not to think," an exhibit that "would be an embarrassment if it went up," and one that "works exactly against NPS's new thinking." Pitcaithley had written Superintendent Martha B. Aikens urging an approach similar to that advocated by the Ad Hoc Historians. "The potential for interpreting Washington's residence and slavery on the site," he wrote, "presents the National Park Service with several exciting opportunities." The president's house, he prodded, should be explained and interpreted, and "the juxtaposition of slave quarters (George Washington's slave quarters, no less) and the Liberty Bell" provided "some stirring interpretive possibilities."

> The contradiction in the founding of the country
> between freedom and slavery becomes palpable
> when one actually crosses through a slave quarters
> site when entering a shrine to a major symbol of the
> abolition movement. . . . How better to establish
> the proper historical context for understanding the
> Liberty Bell than by talking about the institution of
> slavery? And not the institution as generalized phe-
> nomenon, but as lived by George Washington's
> own slaves. The fact that Washington's slaves Her-
> cules and Oney Judge sought and gained freedom
> from this very spot gives us interpretive opportuni-
> ties other historic sites can only long for. This jux-

taposition is an interpretive gift that can make the Liberty Bell "experience" much more meaningful to the visiting public. We will have missed a real educational opportunity if we do not act on this possibility.[10]

Under this cudgeling, which was complemented by a barrage of negative press commentary, including a long *New York Times* article on April 20, the INHP superintendent huddled with her staff and regional supervisors. Abandoning their former approach of conceding as little as possible, they agreed to revisit the issue. With Pitcaithley mediating, the entire exhibit was now to be vetted, rethought, and revised. It was agreed that the breathless and uncomplicated prose relating the history of freedom that the bell symbolized should be toned down, while the issue of freedom in a democracy built on slave foundations would be a central theme in the exhibit; that the treatment of the president's house outside the pavilion would be interpreted with attention to the enslaved Africans and indentured servants who toiled there; and that the Park Service would rewrite the script and send it out for review by noted scholars of the African-American experience and the history of liberty in America. David Hollenberg, associate northeast regional director of the Park Service, pledged, "We are looking at the bell as a symbol of an ongoing continuous struggle for liberty rather than [a symbol] of liberty attained."

A team of IHNP staffers, including Doris Fanelli, Coxey Toogood, and Joe Becton, none of whom had been given an opportunity to help shape the original script, worked with the Ad Hoc Historians in a cooperative effort to produce a major revision, which then went out to several scholars, as the Park Service's General Management Plan requires. Replies brought further changes to the script. It was then on its way toward a final review from the Ad Hoc Historians group.

"The paradox of slavery in a land of the free will be a major exhibition theme when the $12.6 million Liberty Bell Center . . . opens next spring," reported the *Inquirer* on August 11. "The text of the exhibition . . . has been completely reworked over the last three months and is nearing completion, according to NPS officials." The completion took another ten weeks, characterized by a new spirit of collaboration between INHP staffers and the Ad Hoc Historians.

With the exhibits to be mounted inside the Liberty Bell Center overhauled, the focus now shifted outside— to the site of the president's house and its interpretation. It was here that the intervention of black Philadelphians (who constitute about half the city's population) made a crucial difference. On July 3, 2002, hundreds of African

Americans demonstrated at the Liberty Bell site. The protest had been organized by the Avenging the Ancestors Coalition, headed by Michael Coard, a black lawyer and urban activist. Another group, the African People's Solidarity Committee, joined a letter-writing campaign and a petition that marshaled several thousand signatures calling for a monument to commemorate Washington's slaves.[11]

While historians and institution leaders pecking away at their computers got media attention, it was the thousands of black Philadelphians speaking with their feet that pushed the movement onto new ground.

In what turned out to be a key move, Congressman Chaka Fattah introduced an amendment to the 2003 budget of the Department of the Interior requiring that the Park Service report to Congress about an appropriate commemoration of the president's house and the slaves who had toiled there. The Appropriations Committee, which oversees the National Park Service funding, voted unanimously for the Fattah amendment. Shortly, the Multicultural Affairs Congress, a division of the Philadelphia Convention and Visitors Bureau, joined the call for a "prominent monument or memorial" fixing in the public memory the contributions of Washington's slaves to the early years of the new republic. Many believed that this would make Philadelphia a premier destination for

"Conjectural Ground Plan of the President's House in Philadelphia,"
superimposed on Liberty Bell Center. The slave quarters and
"Servants' Hall" shown on the outline are conjectural in the ground
plan of the Morris mansion that served as the executive mansion
for presidents Washington and Adams. Courtesy of the Independence
Hall Association: www.ushistory.org. Ground plan and
photograph © 2001 Edward Lawler Jr.

African-American visitors. The City Council followed
suit with a resolution endorsing this plan.[12]

By the fall of 2002 INHP and the northeastern regional leaders agreed that the executive mansion, and the
people who had lived and worked there, deserved commemoration in the grassy space over which visitors would

walk to enter the new Liberty Bell Center. Two design firms were commissioned to work on a plan. On January 14, 2003, the Park Service unveiled plans for the outside exhibits that millions would see, including physical representations of the president's house—a partial footprint of it, perhaps in slate; side walls detailing the presidencies of George Washington and John Adams; stories of the free, unfree, and partially free people who labored there; the history of slavery in Philadelphia and in the nation at large; material on the emergence of the free black community in Philadelphia and the struggle to dismantle the house of slavery, represented by a breach in the wall through which the enslaved figuratively escaped; and, finally, sculptures of Oney Judge and Hercules, two of Washington's slaves who had gained their freedom by fleeing their master just before the end of his presidency. Michael Coard, leader of the Avenging the Ancestors Coalition, applauded the designs, predicting that "our little Black boys and girls [will] beam with pride when they walk through Independence Mall and witness the true history of America and their brave ancestors."[13]

The fight was not yet over. In the meantime, the shimmering glass-and-steel Liberty Bell Center opened on October 9, 2003. Long lines of visitors went through security checks to see the revered Liberty Bell. For the first time in its history, touching, kissing, and caressing the bell was no longer allowed, a Park Service preservationist decision dictated by the fear that the bell might be loved to death.

With black Philadelphians now highly energized, their long-simmering resentments about the INHP's policies and procedures rushed to the surface. But the decision to move forward, fully backed by a new INHP superintendent, Mary Bomar (later to become director of the National Park Service), began to clear the air. Adopting NPS's Civic Engagement Plan, INHP held public meetings in collaboration with the Ad Hoc Historians to discuss the design and content of the exhibits outside the Liberty Bell Center. Behind the scenes the many constituent parts of the public that had become involved worked with INHP to realize the revised plan. A high-spirited overflow crowd gathered in October 2004 to see what thirty-two months of contention, confrontation, and cooperation had accomplished. It was the Philadelphia version of a New England town meeting, and nobody present thought it was a tame affair. But by the end of the day the finish line was in sight. The city's mayor had already promised $1.5 million for the outside exhibits, and INHP's superintendent now promised to find ways to raise another $3 million. In response to urgings to include African-American architects and planners, the call went out for a design firm competition. In the meantime, INHP agreed to mark the site of the president's house with temporary interpretive wayside panels; produce a leaflet with more information on those who toiled there; and provide first-person interpretations of Oney Judge, Martha Washington's personal slave, and Hercules, the Washingtons' prize chef. It now seemed clear that the Liberty Bell would toll for all on this history-rich site.

After an extended design competition, in late February 2007 Kelly/Maiello Architects and Planners were given the commission. Further delays were in store when, under new pressure, INHP agreed to do archaeological excavations of the thirteen thousand square feet of space outside the Liberty Bell Center in order to find traces of the lives of those who toiled for Presidents Washington and Adams. Thousands of spectators passed through a viewing station during the six months when hard-hatted archaeologists dug, sifted, dusted, and marked artifacts recovered from the many privy shafts and wells dug on the property when it was Robert Morris's mansion. Schematic designs were submitted to INHP in October 2008, and the exhibits were scheduled for unveiling in 2010.

The Liberty Bell, resting comfortably in its new home, awaits the completion of the exhibits in its front and side yards. At that point, the site's tangled history will become one of the most fascinating "contact zones" in the nation's historic sites. To museum professionals a contact zone is

The Liberty Bell in the new Liberty Bell Center, 2003. Courtesy
Independence National Historical Park

one in which people arrive from different backgrounds
and experiences to find themselves looking at pieces of
the past (or pieces of art); such a place offers no simple an-
swers and often suggests competing interpretations. This

is what NPS's chief historian had hoped for when he called for revamping the Liberty Bell exhibits as they were about to be installed in their original form:

> The text assumes that the inspirational message of the Bell has resulted in a steady progression of the expansion of liberty throughout the United States and the world. . . . It assumes there is only one interpretation of the message. . . . How much more interesting (and useful) the exhibit would be if it acknowledged that the "liberty road" has been filled with potholes and obstacles and while the United States has a more expansive definition of freedom and liberty than it did one hundred or even fifty years ago, the struggle is not over. There is a long tradition of assumed freedoms sliding backward on occasion.[14]

Today, about 1.5 million visitors a year enter the Liberty Bell Center. Some walk through the exhibits slowly, tarrying to look at particular photographs, artifacts, memorabilia, and other items. Others move quickly, eager to get to the bell at the south end of the building. There the cameras begin to click. They have seen America's greatest historical icon. Meanwhile, $10.6 million has been secured for the construction, maintenance, and programming of the exhibits outside the center. When the President's

House Memorial is completed by July 4, 2010, perhaps 2 million visitors a year will see the Liberty Bell in all of its many stages of life, in all of its triumphs and travails, in all of the ways it has moved and inspired people from nearly every country in the world. Now it is truly everyone's bell.

Notes

Introduction

1. New Liberty Bell Center, unit 12. See Ernest Morris, *Bells of All Nations* (London: Hale, 1951) for the importance of bells in human society.
2. *San Diego Union*, November 12, 1915; Frank Morton Todd, *The Story of the Exposition, Being the Official History of the International Celebration Held at San Francisco in 1915 . . .*, 5 vols. (New York: G. P. Putnam's Sons, 1921), 3: 90.

ONE
Beginnings

1. Charles M. Boland, *Ring in the Jubilee: The Epic of America's Liberty Bell* (Riverside, CT: Chatham, 1973), 12.
2. Ibid., 25.
3. Ibid., 41.
4. Edward Straham, ed., *A Century After: Picturesque Glimpses of Philadelphia and Pennsylvania . . .* (Philadelphia: Allen, Lane, and Scott, 1875), 14, quoted in John C. Paige, *The Liberty Bell: A Special History Study*, ed. David C. Kimball (Denver: Denver

Service Center and Independence National Historical Park, c. 1973), 85; hereafter, NPS Study.

5. Boland, *Ring in the Jubilee*, 40.
6. Ibid., 46.
7. Charles Norris to James Wright, March 29, 1753; J. C. Wyler, "Four Gossipy Letters," *Pennsylvania Magazine of History and Biography* 39 (1915), 464.
8. Norris to Robert Charles, April 14, 1753, quoted in Boland, *Ring in the Jubilee*, 49.
9. Boland, *Ring in the Jubilee*, 51–52.
10. Ibid., 55.
11. Ibid., 58–59; NPS Study, 15.
12. Boland, *Ring in the Jubilee*, 60.
13. Ibid., 61.
14. Ibid., 63.
15. Both sources are quoted in NPS Study, 18. It is possible that the State House bell did not ring at all on July 8 because the rotting steeple made it dangerous to ring the bell. See Charlene Mires, *Independence Hall in American Memory* (Philadelphia: University of Pennsylvania Press, 2002), 290–91n63, for evidence of this. This possibility is also raised in NPS Study, 18.
16. NPS Study, 21.
17. Boland, *Ring in the Jubilee*, 90.
18. Quoted in Mires, *Independence Hall in American Memory*, 42.
19. Gary B. Nash, *First City: Philadelphia and the Forging of Historical Memory* (Philadelphia: University of Pennsylvania Press, 2002), 2.
20. Ibid., 2.
21. Ibid., 7.
22. Mires, *Independence Hall in American Memory*, 73–75.
23. Boland, *Ring in the Jubilee*, 94.
24. Charles S. Keyser, *The Liberty Bell, Independence Hall, Philadelphia, 1893* (Philadelphia, 1893), 26.
25. Unidentified source from Independence National Historical Park files.
26. Nash, *First City*, for details; Boland, *Ring in the Jubilee*, 52.
27. *Register of Pennsylvania*, September 26, 1829, quoted in Mires, *Independence Hall in American Memory*, 77.

TWO
The Bell Becomes an Icon

1. Thompson Westcott, *The Official Guide Book to Philadelphia: A New Handbook for Strangers and Citizens* (Philadelphia: Porter and Coates, 1875), 101; John Fanning Watson, *Annals of Philadelphia*, ed. Willis P. Hazard, 3 vols. (Philadelphia: J. M. Stoddart, 1879), 3: 209; *New York Times*, July 9, 1935.

2. John Sartain, *The Reminiscences of a Very Old Man, 1808–1897* (New York: D. Appleton, 1899), 123; John C. Paige, *The Liberty Bell: A Special History Study*, ed. David C. Kimball (Denver: Denver Service Center and Independence National Historical Park, c. 1973), 27; hereafter, NPS Study.

3. *New York Times*, July 16, 1911.

4. *Annals of Philadelphia*, 3: 209; *Public Ledger*, quoted in NPS Study, 30; Charles M. Boland, *Ring in the Jubilee: The Epic of America's Liberty Bell* (Riverside, CT: Chatham, 1973), 97.

5. *Anti-Slavery Record* 1, no. 2 (1835).

6. *Liberator*, November 8, 1839, p. 180; NPS Study, 80–81, for New York City and Boston publications.

7. NPS Study, 81, quoting *The Liberty Bell* (Boston: Anti-Slavery Fair, 1842), 60–61.

8. Boland, *Ring in the Jubilee*, 104; NPS Study, 82.

9. *American Daily Advertiser*, March 5, 1828, p. 2, quoted in NPS Study, 80.

10. William Duane, ed., *Extracts from the Diary of Christopher Marshall* (New York: New York Times, 1969 reprint), 82.

11. Benson J. Lossing, *Pictorial Field-Book of the Revolution*, 2 vols. (New York: Harper and Brothers, 1851–52), 2: 263–64.

12. Ibid., 2: 272–73, 285.

13. George G. Foster, "Philadelphia in Slices," ed. George Rogers Taylor, *Pennsylvania Magazine of History and Biography* 93 (1969), 54, 72, cited in NPS Study, 31; R. A. Smith, *Philadelphia as It Is in 1852 . . .* (Philadelphia: Lindsay and Blaketon, 1852), 30, cited in NPS Study, 84.

14. *Public Ledger*, December 25, 1851; July 13, 1853.

15. Quoted in Charlene Mires, *Independence Hall in American Memory* (Philadelphia: University of Pennsylvania Press, 2002), 94.

16. Quoted ibid., 97, 99.
17. *Public Ledger*, April 28, 1848, cited in NPS Study, 31; Mires, *Independence Hall in American Memory*, 103–5.
18. NPS Study, 32; Charles MacKay, *Life and Liberty in America . . .*, 2 vols. (London, 1859), 1: 119, quoted in NPS Study, 33.
19. *Graham's Magazine* 44, no. 6 (June 1854).
20. William Chambers, *Things as They Are in America* (Philadelphia: Lippincott, Grambo, 1854), 308, cited in NPS Study, 84; David W. Belisle, *History of Independence Hall: From the Earliest Period to the Present Time* (Philadelphia: James Challen, 1859), 81–82.
21. *Philadelphia Inquirer*, April 1, 1926. For Work's "Ring the Bell," see www.jsward.com/shanty/StrikeTheBell/RingTheBell.html.
22. *Philadelphia Inquirer*, April 25, 1865.
23. "Liberty Bell Quotes," USHistory.com, http://www.ushistory .org/LibertyBell/quotes.html.
24. Quoted in Mary D. Alexander, *Andrew McNair and the Liberty Bell, 1776* (Chicago: University of Chicago Press, 1929), 8–11.
25. NPS Study, 84–85.
26. Cited in NPS Study, 85.
27. NPS Study, 33–34.
28. Quoted by Arthur H. Frazier, "Henry Seybert and the Centennial Clock and Bell at Independence Hall," *Pennsylvania Magazine of History and Biography* 102 (1978), 47–48.
29. NPS Study, 86–87.
30. *Harpers's Weekly*, July 15, 1876, 579.
31. NPS Study, 85.
32. Quoted in Karal Ann Marling, *George Washington Slept Here: Colonial Revivals and American Culture, 1876–1986* (Cambridge: Harvard University Press, 1988), 30.
33. Frank M. Etting, *An Historical Account of the Old State House of Pennsylvania Now Known as the Hall of Independence* (Philadelphia: James R. Osgood, 1876), 88.
34. Gary B. Nash, *First City: Philadelphia and the Forging of Historical Memory* (Philadelphia: University of Pennsylvania Press, 2002), 280–82; Mires, *Independence Hall in American Memory*, 132.
35. Nash, *First City*, 275, quoting *Evening Bulletin*, July 5, 1876.
36. *Public Ledger*, April 14, 1877; June 27, 1877.
37. Victor Rosewater, *The Liberty Bell: Its History and Significance*

(New York: D. Appleton, 1926), 138–39; David Kimball, *Venerable Relic: The Story of the Liberty Bell* (Philadelphia: Eastern National Park and Monument Association, 1989), 68; NPS Study, 35.

THREE

On the Road with the Bell

1. Charlene Mires, *Independence Hall in American Memory* (Philadelphia: University of Pennsylvania Press, 2002), 150.
2. John C. Paige, *The Liberty Bell: A Special History Study*, ed. David C. Kimball (Denver: Denver Service Center and Independence National Historical Park, c. 1973), 35; hereafter, NPS Study.
3. Ibid., 36.
4. Charles M. Boland, *Ring in the Jubilee: The Epic of America's Liberty Bell* (Riverside, CT: Chatham, 1973), 107–9.
5. Boland (ibid., 109) says this was in Virginia, but that seems impossible.
6. Willis J. Abbott, *Watching the World Go By* (Boston: Little, Brown, 1934), 10–11.
7. Robert Rydell, *All the World's a Fair: Visions of Empire at American International Expositions, 1876–1916* (Chicago: University of Chicago Press, 1984), 80–81.
8. Victor Rosewater, *The Liberty Bell: Its History and Significance* (New York: Appleton, 1926), 154–56.
9. Stuart McConnell, "Reading the Flag: A Reconsideration of the Patriotic Cults of the 1890s," in *Bonds of Affection: Americans Define Their Patriotism*, ed. John Bodnar (Princeton: Princeton University Press, 1996), 102–19. For a broad consideration of commemoration, national identity, and patriotism, see the essays in John Gillis, ed., *Commemorations: The Politics of National Identity* (Princeton: Princeton University Press, 1994).
10. Mires, *Independence Hall in American Memory*, 136–38; Gary B. Nash, *First City: Philadelphia and the Forging of Historical Memory* (Philadelphia: University of Pennsylvania Press, 2002), 303–9.
11. Rosewater, *Liberty Bell*, 157.
12. April 25, 1893, quoted ibid., 158.
13. Quoted ibid., 159.

14. Quoted in Mires, *Independence Hall in American Memory*, 156.
15. *New York Times*, April 28, 1893.
16. "Chicago's Royal Welcome," Philadelphia *Public Ledger*, May 1, 1893, quoted in NPS Study, 38; Rosewater, *Liberty Bell*, 160.
17. From unidentified newspaper clipping in Independence National Historical Park files; also see Halsey C. Ives, *The Dream City: A Portfolio of Photographic Views of the World's Columbian Expos* (St. Louis: N. D. Thompson, 1893).
18. NPS Study, 89.
19. World's Columbian Exposition of 1893, www.hydepark.org/historicpres/ColumbianExp.htm#mystery.
20. "Oration Delivered at the Invitation of the City of Chicago . . . on the Fourth Day of July, 1893," *Pennsylvania Magazine of History and Biography* 17 (1894), 49–55.
21. Christopher Robert Reed, *"All the World Is Here!" The Black Presence at White City* (Bloomington: Indiana University Press, 2000).
22. *Public Ledger*, November 2, 1893.
23. "Pennsylvania's Ovation," *Public Ledger*, Nov. 4, 1893, p. 8 for both Reading and Allentown.
24. "Our Liberty's Return," *Public Ledger*, November 7, 1893; Rosewater, *Liberty Bell*, 163.
25. *Public Ledger*, October 24, 1893, cited in NPS Study, 40.
26. *Philadelphia Sunday Inquirer*, August 31, 1895.
27. Rosewater, *Liberty Bell*, 166–67, quoting *Public Ledger*, October 7, 1895.
28. Quoted in Rydell, *All the World's a Fair*, 73; Rosewater, *Liberty Bell*, 167.
29. Quoted in Rosewater, *Liberty Bell*, 170.
30. Quoted ibid., 173.
31. Mary Field Parton, ed., *The Autobiography of Mother Jones* (Chicago: C. H. Kerr, 1990), 73–83.
32. For a powerful explication of the organizing and assembling of the ethnographic exhibits, with exotically presented indigenous people from all corners of the world, see Nancy J. Parezo and Don D. Fowler, *Anthropology Goes to the Fair: The 1904 Louisiana Purchase Exposition* (Lincoln: University of Nebraska Press, 2007). The quotation is on p. 10.

33. James H. Lambert, *Pennsylvania at the World's Fair, St. Louis* (Philadelphia: Pennsylvania Commission, 1904), 1: 354.
34. *Public Ledger,* April 16, 1909; *New York Times,* February 16, 17, 1909.
35. Frank Morton Todd, *The Story of the Exposition, Being the Official History of the International Celebration Held at San Francisco in 1915 . . .,* 5 vols. (New York: G. P. Putnam's Sons, 1921), 5: 358.
36. Ibid., 359–60.
37. Jordan to Chief, Bureau of City Property, November 16, 1914, quoted in NPS Study, 91.
38. Todd, *Story of the Exposition,* 5: 358.
39. *Public Ledger,* February 13, 1915, quoted in Rosewater, *Liberty Bell,* 179–80.
40. Rosewater, *Liberty Bell,* 185.
41. *New York Times,* March 31, 1915; *Philadelphia Evening Ledger,* March 25, 1915.
42. *Philadelphia Inquirer,* April 1, 1915.
43. Mires, *Independence Hall in American Memory,* 154–55, quoting from *Rocky Mountain News,* July 11, 1915, and other sources.
44. *Seattle Post-Intelligencer,* July 15, 1915.
45. Todd, *Story of the Exposition,* 3: 90.
46. Quoted ibid., 3: 92.
47. *Philadelphia Ledger,* July 31, 1915.
48. Ibid.
49. Todd, *Story of the Exposition,* 5: 358.
50. *San Diego Union,* November 13, 1915.
51. *Philadelphia Public Ledger,* November 27, 1915.

FOUR

The Liberty Bell in War and Peace

1. *New York Times,* June 13, 1917.
2. *Public Ledger,* September 8, 1918, magazine section, 2. Duke University soon adopted the Blue Devils as their mascot.
3. Victor Rosewater, *The Liberty Bell: Its History and Significance* (New York: Appleton, 1926), 189, from *Public Ledger,* Nov. 26, 1917.
4. *New York Times,* October 27, 1918; November 4, 1928.

5. *Troy* (N.Y.) *Record*, September 7, 1948; http://en.wikipedia.org/wiki/Meneely_bell_foundry.

6. John C. Paige, *The Liberty Bell: A Special History Study*, ed. David C. Kimball (Denver: Denver Service Center and Independence National Historical Park, c. 1973), 54; hereafter, NPS Study.

7. *Philadelphia Evening Bulletin*, July 8, 1922; *New York Times*, July 14, 1922; March 1, 1939.

8. NPS Study, 58; Charlene Mires, *Independence Hall in American Memory* (Philadelphia: University of Pennsylvania Press, 2002), 167.

9. *Philadelphia Inquirer*, July 5, 1934; July 5, 1935; NPS Study, 62–63.

10. Mires, *Independence Hall in American Memory*, 170.

11. *New York Times*, September 19, October 12, 1924.

12. *New York Times*, January 23, 1925.

13. *Philadelphia Inquirer*, April 22, 1936; *New York Times*, June 23, 1936.

14. "A Fantasy! How America Upset a Nazi Invasion and Forced Hitler to Surrender in Independence Hall," *Philadelphia Inquirer*, November 3, 1940.

15. *Philadelphia Inquirer*, October 24, 1940.

16. Frances Rogers and Alice Beard, *Old Liberty Bell* (Philadelphia: J. B. Lippincott, 1942).

17. Mires, *Independence Hall in American Memory*, 199–200; *Philadelphia Bulletin*, May 26, 1943; *Philadelphia Inquirer*, April 28, 1943.

18. *Philadelphia Record*, July 4, 1942.

19. NPS Study, 67.

20. Ibid.

21. Liberty Belle: B-17 Flying Fortress, http://www.libertyfoundation.org/index.html; Grissom Air Museum Web site, grissomairmuseum.com/home.html.

22. Grissom Air Museum site.

23. Mires, *Independence Hall in American Memory*, 227.

24. *New York Times*, October 30, 1950; July 9, 1951; November 2, 1952.

25. *New York Times*, November 7, 1950.

26. *Philadelphia Inquirer*, October 5, 1950.

27. *Observer,* July 14, 1958, quoted in NPS Study, 99.
28. *Philadelphia Inquirer,* June 19, 1930; March 3, 1939.
29. *Philadelphia Bulletin,* February 2, 1960.
30. *New York Times,* October 5, 1951.
31. Mires, *Independence Hall in American Memory,* 204.
32. Ibid., 207.
33. *Philadelphia Inquirer,* September 23, 1963.
34. *Evening Bulletin* and *Philadelphia Inquirer,* September 23, 1963.
35. *Philadelphia Inquirer,* April 4, 1965; *Evening Bulletin,* February 16, 17, 1965.
36. *Philadelphia Inquirer,* March 12, 1965; *New York Times,* March 13, 1965; *Philadelphia Bulletin,* March 13, 1965, quoted in Mires, *Independence Hall in American Memory,* 249.
37. Mires, *Independence Hall in American Memory,* 254; *Philadelphia Bulletin,* May 15, 1967.
38. *Time,* May 4, 1970.
39. *Philadelphia Inquirer,* April 4, 1965.
40. *Philadelphia Inquirer,* September 11, 12, 15, 1969.
41. Constance M. Greiff, *Independence: The Creation of a National Park* (University of Pennsylvania Press, 1987), chapter 2.
42. Ibid.
43. *Philadelphia Evening Bulletin,* January 6, 1959.
44. *Philadelphia Inquirer,* February 4, 1972.
45. *New York Times,* January 1, 1976.
46. *Philadelphia Bulletin,* February 25, 1968.
47. *Philadelphia Inquirer,* November 20, 1970.
48. NPS Study, 99.
49. Mires, *Independence Hall in American Memory,* 276.
50. Ibid., 278.
51. Ibid., 274; numbers provided by David Sillery, Public Affairs, Independence National Historical Park, to Gary B. Nash via email, October 6, 2008.

FIVE
Everyone's Liberty Bell

1. *Washington Times, Philadelphia Inquirer, New York Times,* April 1, 1996.

2. Victor Rosewater, *The Liberty Bell: Its History and Significance* (New York: Appleton, 1926), 217.
3. Quoted ibid., 219–20.
4. *Philadelphia Inquirer,* July 3, 1898.
5. For the history of the site, see Edward Lawler, "The President's House in Philadelphia: The Rediscovery of a Lost Landmark," *Pennsylvania Magazine of History and Biography* 126 (2002), 5–95; Edward Lawler, "The President's House Revisited," *Pennsylvania Magazine of History and Biography* 129 (2005), 371–409.
6. Dwight Pitcaithley, "'A Cosmic Threat': The National Park Service Addresses the Causes of the American Civil War," in *Slavery and Public History: The Tough Stuff of American Memory,* ed. James Oliver Horton and Lois E. Horton (New York: New Press, 2006), 169–86.
7. Quoted in Gary B. Nash, "For Whom Will the Liberty Bell Toll? From Controversy to Cooperation," in Horton and Horton, *Slavery and Public History,* 74–101. The following pages are adapted from this essay. "The National Park Service and Civil Engagement" can be viewed at www.nps.gov/civic. The American Association of Museums added momentum with its *Mastering Civic Engagement: A Challenge to Museums* (Washington, DC: American Association of Museums, 2002).
8. Jill Ogline, "'Creating Dissonance for the Visitor': The Heart of the Liberty Bell Controversy," *Public Historian* 216 (2004), 52, 55.
9. For this coverage and that outlined in the next three paragraphs, see *Philadelphia Inquirer,* March 26, 27, 31. Dozens of other newspaper articles, op-ed essays, and letters to the editor can be viewed at www.ushistory.org/presidentshouse.
10. Pitcaithley to Martha Atkins, April 3, 2002, quoted with Pitcaithley's permission.
11. *Philadelphia Inquirer,* June 11, 2002.
12. *Philadelphia Inquirer,* July 3, 4, August 11. My essay in Horton and Horton, *Slavery and Public History,* provides greater detail on the course of the debate and the actions taken by the National Park Service.
13. A series of articles on the design and the design itself can be viewed at www.ushistory.org/presidentshouse/plans/jan2003/index.htm. See also Doris Devine Fanelli, "History, Commem-

oration, and an Interdisciplinary Approach to Interpreting the President's House Site," *Pennsylvania Magazine of History and Biography* 129 (2005), 445–60. This issue of *PMHB* has other essays on the debate by Edward Lawler Jr., Michael Coard, Sharon Ann Holt, and others.

14. Dwight Pitcaithley to Dennis Reidenbach, May 2, 2002, quoted with Pitcaithley's permission.

Acknowledgments

Two years ago, Mark Crispin Miller, Icons of America series editor at Yale University Press, suggested I write a book on the Liberty Bell. To Mark, and to Sandra Dijkstra, my literary agent who pushed me ahead on this idea, I am most grateful for dispatching me on such a pleasurable journey of research and writing.

In working on this book, I was assisted at UCLA's National Center for History in the Schools by Marian Olivas, program coordinator at the Center, and undergraduate work-study student Laura Mills. Karen Stevens, the archivist at the library of Independence National Historical Park (INHP), was indispensable in steering me through the Liberty Bell archives, which include newspaper clippings, a trove of photographs, and assorted materials relating to the bell's history. Steve Sitarski, chief of interpretation and visitors services at INHP, also provided information on the recent history of the Liberty Bell.

Charlene Mires, Villanova University, gave the manuscript of this book a thorough reading and offered many valuable suggestions. Two readers commissioned by Yale University Press, Stanley Katz at Princeton and Bob Rydell at Montana State, graciously commented on the manuscript and helped me improve it. Assistant editor Sarah Miller at Yale was helpful in hastening the project along, and Dan Heaton proved to be a supportive and hawk-eyed manuscript editor. I am grateful to him for helping me make the book as free of errors and infelicities as possible.

Index

abolitionists, 5–6, 35–40, 49, 57, 104
Abu-Jamal, Mumia, 180
Adams, John, 18, 27, 212, 214
Address to the Negro People (Walker), 36
Ad Hoc Historians, 201–2, 204, 207, 209, 213
advertising, 185–86, 196
African Americans, xiii, 49, 50, 59, 81, 100, 203; civil rights movement and, 165–69; Columbian Exposition and, 95; Liberty Bell and, 2, 144, 165, 168, 209–11, 212, 213; National Freedom Day and, 164, 165; violence against, 82, 100, 167. *See also* slavery
African Methodist Episcopal Church, 81
African People's Solidarity Committee, 210

Aikens, Martha B., 207, 208
Ali, Muhammad, 192
Allentown (Pa.), 19, 96
American Friends Service Committee, 146
American Historical Association, 77
Americanization, 85, 110
American Party, 55–56
American Revolution, xii, 13–20, 42, 46–47, 64, 71, 77
Anaconda Copper, 185, 187
Annals of Philadelphia and Pennsylvania in the Olden Times (Watson), 34
Anthony, Susan B., 72–74, 115
anti-Communism, 154–55, 162, 165. *See also* Cold War
Anti-Slavery Convention of American Women, 37
antislavery movement. *See* abolitionists

CPSIA information can be obtained at www.ICGtesting.com
Printed in the USA
BVOW04s2311221014

371953BV00002B/8/P